KNIGHTSTONE

The Story of Weston-super-Mare's 'Island' Theatre

Jonathan Shorney

redcliffe

First published in 2015 by Redcliffe Press Ltd.,
81g Pembroke Road, Bristol BS8 3EA

www.redcliffepress.co.uk
info@redcliffepress.co.uk

© Jonathan Shorney

ISBN 978-1-908326-72-0
British Library Cataloguing-in-Publication Data
A catalogue record for this book is available from the British Library

Design and typesetting by Stephen Morris www.stephen-morris.co.uk
Set in Times 10.5/13
Printed by Hobbs the Printers Ltd, Totton

Front cover: Detail from *View of Knightstone from the Promenade* by Warren Storey,
head of Weston-super-Mare School of Art, 1950-1984.

Contents

Introduction 5

Status Symbol 8

Electric Moving Pictures 26

The Three Musketeers 51

Variety Heyday 71

New Look 92

Cabaret Style 117

Dilapidation 141

Appendix: List of shows 151

Acknowledgements 174

Index 175

Weston-super-Mare in 1903, before the building of the Grand Pier and Winter Gardens Pavilion.

Introduction

I never went to Knightstone Theatre – and no one else would have either had it been up to my great-great uncle. Jesse Shorney was a founding father of modern Weston-super-Mare, one of its 18 Victorian Town Commissioners who had migrated from his native Cannington by standing in an open railway truck as a third-class passenger with the proverbial half-crown in his pocket. As a builder he had embraced the town's pioneering spirit with houses, High Street shops and Stuckey's Bank to his name. But he opposed the siting of a pavilion – as it was then known – intended as a wet-weather refuge on an exposed 'island' half-a-mile from the milling crowds. A pavilion was a status symbol, long desired by a resort being dubbed 'Bristol's Brighton'. Major players such as Blackpool, Bournemouth and Llandudno had them and locally Ilfracombe was luring custom away with an impressive iron and glass structure inspired by the Crystal Palace in south London. But one on Knightstone, at the northern end of Weston Bay? The *Weston Gazette* reckoned the entire promenade from Regent Street to the 'island' would need a glass roof before anyone would be persuaded to seek shelter there. Jesse knew enough about the trade to realise that what was proposed – a glorified greenhouse for band performances – wouldn't have lasted five minutes against the fury of the sea.

The new Urban District Council, which replaced the Commissioners, nevertheless pressed ahead with their flagship project, built eventually of far sturdier stuff to withstand the harsh coastal elements. It was now suited to an enhanced repertoire of drama, musicals, opera and concerts for visitors who more than doubled Weston's 20,000 population. Not that the town had lacked amusements. The beach was thick with tented shows, stalls and sand artists and Birnbeck Pier boasted a switchback railway and water chute. But those were for excursionists down for the day or the steamer crowd over from South Wales – the sort who 'rode in the traps and sang ribald songs' according to one councillor, who hoped the pavilion would attract a better class of clientele.

For a while it was popular. Paul Robeson, Dame Clara Butt and famous Shakespearean Sir Frank Benson were among the early stars. But the shine soon came off Weston's showpiece attraction. It struggled to attract high-calibre productions and became under-used and heavily loss-making. It resorted four times to showing films to try to make ends meet but couldn't compete with well-appointed cinemas that sprang up in the town centre – still less with the Grand Pier with its own magnificent theatre. The pavilion became a white elephant and a ratepayers' association was formed to demand action to stem the losses.

And that, you might say, was Act One of the building's story. Act Two was unrecognisably different. In the unlikely setting of the Second World War it was spectacularly re-invented as Knightstone Theatre, thanks to the exceptional entrepreneurial skills of a few talented individuals. They ran it as a number one circuit variety house that starred Max Miller, Robb Wilton, Frankie Howerd, Norman Wisdom and Morecambe and Wise, and formed one of the country's finest repertory companies. Even in the biggest seaside town between Lancashire and Land's End the theatre punched well above its weight. There were dazzling professional and legendary amateur pantomimes and polished productions by Weston's Operatic and Dramatic Societies.

Later the council re-took control and resident summer shows were presented. Those productions – *Gaytime* and *Let's Make a Night of It* – in the 1950s and 1960s ran to 18 weeks with packed houses that could only be dreamed of a few years later. It was the British seaside holiday heyday and show posters covered the town. Different programmes were staged during a season and some residents saw them all – many times over. The number of staying visitors began to slide but fans who regarded the stars almost as old friends returned year after year.

By the 1970s Knightstone was struggling, along with every other theatre that had survived the decimation wrought by television and cheap package holidays. It ditched its off-season schedule, or what little of it that remained, and converted to a sort of cabaret club open in summer only. This enjoyed varying degrees of success depending on how big a name had been booked. By now fewer crowd-pulling entertainers were available – and Knightstone could barely afford those who were. The resort had become a paradise for trippers who went home before shows began. Many who did stay spent comfortable evenings in now fully licensed guest houses, or hotels that had installed colour televisions.

Weston agonised over what to do for the best – whether to give up on the theatre and risk losing even more visitors or throw good money after bad on an old building with little return at the box office. The town could ill afford to keep the crumbling landmarks of its tourist industry, the lifeblood of its economy, yet could ill afford not to. The premises limped on in different guises until 1991 and today only the façade remains as part of a housing development.

Knightstone might have lacked the architectural grandeur and welcoming gilt and crimson plush of opulent, purpose-built theatres. At times it was an ice box – once the entertainments manager presented a showgirl who had complained about the cold with a beautifully wrapped hot-water bottle. But it had its own charm, a unique sea-front location (it was misremembered by some former artistes as an end-of-the-pier theatre) and, in its day, audiences in carefree mood who thought nothing of spending almost every night of their holidays at a show.

Oh to have been among them.

Status Symbol

In an endearing New Year tradition in the early twentieth century the humblest of Weston-super-Mare society wrapped up against the night cold and struggled out to Knightstone 'island'.

The 400 elderly residents, registered as 'deserving poor', were looking forward to the highlight of their year: a feast and entertainment at the pavilion courtesy of the town's freemasons. Instead of the usual austere interior, a festive scene awaited them of wall-mounted animal heads, antlers and mistletoe, while pink shades subdued bright electric light. Removable stalls seating had been stacked away and trestle tables covered with white linen arranged in lines.

The evenings began with the quaintly-deferential business of wiring a pledge of allegiance and best wishes to the King and Queen, a thank-you telegram being received from Buckingham Palace before they went home, once jogging proud memories of a woman who had waved a flag at Queen Victoria's coronation. A roast beef supper was served by black-tied members of St Kew Lodge, led by veteran mason Billy Perrett who had started these 'old folk treats' in the 1880s and was by now older than any of the diners he waited on. Local amateur comics and singers performed on stage, followed by the novelty of a silent film. The night would end with punch, Auld Lang Syne and the National Anthem accompanied by Weston Amateur Orchestra.

Earlier 'treats' had been held in the smaller Victoria Hall in the Boulevard but in 1902 Weston got its gleaming new pavilion and the community could spread its wings on red-letter dates in the social calendar. Elaborate decorations were prepared months in advance for grand military, sporting, hospital and political party balls. A Weston Harriers' Hunt Ball was held in an intricate replica of an Elizabethan courtyard with statue, stone walls and rock garden, while a barn roof strung with ancient hurricane lamps overhung the balcony. An Armistice Day anniversary dance included the bizarre, if not irreverent, special effect of a raiding Zeppelin coming under fire from anti-aircraft guns and machine-gun outposts. At a Shipwrecked Mariners' Society evening, a masthead topped with red light was set up on stage and when the light shone women could ask men for a dance, it being a leap year. Elders and Fyffes

One of the earliest pictures of Knightstone peninsula, dated 1835.

specially imported a banana grove from Jamaica to decorate a Commercial Travellers' Ball. The touring Springboks team, having thrashed a joint Gloucestershire-Somerset side, were forgiven guests at a Weston Rugby Club dance, where flowers, rosettes and lampshades sported the visitors' green and gold colours.

The hall was painstakingly transformed into a Tudor scene of half-timbered houses and shops for a three-day fayre and maske, and for a week-long old English village Christmas market 300 helpers wore lace bodices, bustles, frills, flounces and bonnets to serve in lantern-lit shops tucked under the balcony. Hundreds attended spectacular fancy dress balls and excited crowds huddled outside to watch them arrive. One guest was so convincingly disguised he was turned away by a doorman mistaking him for a labourer from a nearby construction site.

But to find out why this new entertainment house was built a 20-minute walk from the town hall on a dreary clump of rock at the mercy of the sea we must go back a hundred years.

In the early nineteenth century Weston was a lonely fishing village on the Somerset coast and the barren acre-and-a-half island of Knightstone an unlikely stage for anything. Cut off daily by the tide, it was little more than a shelter for discharging coal-boats from South Wales.

Its fortunes changed as the wealthy, who once took therapeutic waters at spa towns, began to pursue good health at the coast, attracted by claims about the healing properties of sea water. Enterprising developers eyed Knightstone as a suitable site for hot and cold baths to catch the prevailing mood. While these were being built, huge human bones were uncovered, giving rise to popular legend that they were of a Roman knight after whom the area was named. However, the word had previously been written as Nightstone and probably derived from the dark limestone once quarried there and used for fireplaces in the grander local houses.

After changing hands several times the island was bought in 1828 by the man who really put it on the map, Dr Edward Long Fox. Fox, a distant relative of engineer Francis Fox who would design two of Weston's railway stations, vastly improved the facilities, believing chemical baths and sea bathing would aid the patients of his privately-run asylum near Bristol. He increased the size of the island behind a new perimeter wall and raised the causeway above high-water level, re-defining Knightstone as a peninsula, a pedantic point to those who went on calling it an island. Of the clutter of buildings, his elegant two-storey Georgian-style bath-house survives to this day. These enhancements helped boost Weston's profile so that by the 1880s it was famed as a fashionable watering-hole with 14,000 residents.

The lord of the manor Cecil Hugh Smyth-Pigott and deputy lord lieutenant John Jeremiah Jackson-Barstow were directors of a company that bought the peninsula in 1891 and carried out further improvements. The 'island' was expanded in area again, unsightly buildings were demolished and the baths upgraded. A bandstand with electric light and 150-seat shelter was constructed but bad weather affected concert attendances.

Bad weather was Weston's Achilles' heel. Since 1882 it had had a glazed Summer and Winter Gardens but this was privately owned and some distance from the front alongside Victoria Hall. In poor conditions visitors complained of little to do and went home early rather than be cooped up in lodgings all day. The Town Commissioners – the ruling body of white-bearded elders established in 1842 – had long desired a sea-front pavilion to afford shelter and entertainment during adverse weather and the off-season but were unlikely to have secured borrowing approval from the

An architect's vision of a pavilion at Knightstone. Elegant but flimsy designs of this sort were rejected because they would not withstand the power of the sea.

Local Government Board. The creation of a Weston-super-Mare Urban District Council in 1894 galvanised town leaders into action. The ideal spot for such a prestigious building was Rogers' Field – where the Winter Gardens Pavilion now stands – but covenants applying to the land would have restricted building height. Other sites were considered: in Birnbeck Road or on a widened promenade at Ellenborough Park or Regent Street, years before a Grand Pier appeared at the latter.

However, the council urgently turned its attention to Knightstone peninsula, fearing it was about to be sold to outsiders who might not have the town's best interests at heart. The owners wanted £14,000 for the property but in hard bargaining agreed to drop the price to £12,000 for 14 days only, an offer eagerly accepted by the council. The decision was not unanimous, one councillor in particular, the Rev William Boyden, a retired Methodist minister, leading the opposition to siting and price. He believed the council was being stampeded into purchase and was the first to predict the pavilion would become a white elephant.

As a Weston-super-Mare Act of Parliament was required for the scheme to go ahead the council seized the opportunity of including other grand ambitions within the same legislation. Soon it was planning a 1,100-yard pier from the peninsula for use by passenger steamers unable to land at the 1867 Birnbeck Pier at low water. A massive lake was to be created along a mile of sea-front from Knightstone to the Sanatorium to solve the exasperating problem of Weston's absent tide, which could ebb more than a mile from the promenade, the Bristol Channel experiencing the world's second-largest tidal range. Glentworth Bay was also to be enclosed by a causeway

11

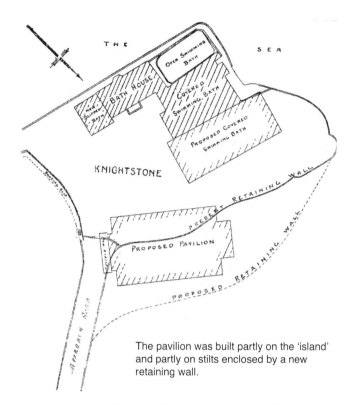

The pavilion was built partly on the 'island' and partly on stilts enclosed by a new retaining wall.

from Knightstone to rocks near Anchor Head to create an adjacent lake. Suddenly the projected £16,500 cost of just land purchase and pavilion leapt to £150,000, the loan charges of which would somehow have to be met along with all other council expenditure from an annual rate limit of 3s 6d, which raised £18,000.

Farcically three low-water piers were now being simultaneously planned – at Knightstone, as an extension to a proposed Grand Pier and at Birnbeck, whose directors belatedly sought to protect their interests. If that was unlikely to impress MPs considering the council's Bill there was also widespread disquiet, fuelled by the town's medical profession, that stagnant lake water could pose a health risk and jeopardise Weston's very reputation as a salubrious resort. In July 1896 a special parliamentary committee approved a pavilion but threw out the pier and lakes sections of the Bill, landing the council with largely abortive legal fees of £4,300.

When a new swimming bath was also proposed for Knightstone, the peninsula blueprint became so crowded that it was decided to build the pavilion partly on pillars on Glentworth sands, shielded by a 15ft high, 400ft long retaining wall. A pavilion design competition was launched, but to the council's horror the president of the Royal Institute of British Architects who judged the entries chose monstrosities that would withstand fierce coastal conditions and rejected far more elegant concepts from other architects. This presented a real quandary as councillors felt morally obliged to appoint the £50 top prize winner, JS Stewart of London, to proceed with the scheme. He was eventually selected but asked to soften the external appearance by replacing brick with Bath stone dressing. Because of press speculation that a Grand Pier with splendid pavilion of its own was imminently expected, Stewart was also told to reduce the number of seats from 2,500 to 1,200.

Bristol firm A Krauss and Son, who had built Weston's magnificent esplanade 16 years earlier, began work in 1899 on the foundations and sea wall, constructed at a cost of £6,300. The contract for the pavilion itself also went to an outsider, a £9,700 quote from HW Pollard of Bridgwater being accepted in June 1900. The only tenderer out of six who was from Weston, Charles Addicott, had submitted the highest figure. With separately priced steel, fitting out, cost increases during construction and professional fees, the final bill came to £21,000. Boyden wryly observed that while capacity had halved, the cost had doubled.

As the building took shape a 50ft-long portico, likened to a cowshed, unexpectedly appeared attached to the main entrance, attributed to an 'amateur architect' at the council tampering with Stewart's drawings amid concern about lack of weather cover for arriving carriages – indeed, it had even been suggested, improbably, that the causeway be glassed over. So awkward was the structure the council considered widening the causeway for extra turning room, but in the end had the thing demolished before the pavilion opened.

The finished building aroused a mixed response. Some considered it too remote from the town centre while others hoped this would deter uncouth excursionists and leave a better class of clientele free to enjoy high standard concerts. The *Western Daily Press* regretted its lack of harmony with the new baths next door, the work of a different architect. One 'disgusted visitor' branded it a combination of factory, workhouse and prison. In fact its complicated style owed more to Renaissance than reformatory. With

A postcard showing the 'unauthorised' portico that was demolished before the pavilion opened. The flèche was removed in the 1930s but is acknowledged by an almost identical one in the modern housing development.

square Italianate towers at each corner, Tuscan columns along two sides and green slate pitched roof punctuated with whimsical flèche, it was an external hotchpotch, but its quizzical front stared at the promenade and beckoned all inside.

From an entrance lobby, double swing doors led through to a 99ft by 67ft spring-floored hall, the largest in Weston, with five-arched bays down both sides. Twelve electric chandeliers, a wondrous spectacle at the time, hung from a barrel-vaulted ceiling. Given its purpose, scant regard had been paid to the needs of music and drama productions. A gilded proscenium framed a surprisingly small stage, just 27ft wide and 18ft deep, from where steps led down to four basic dressing-rooms. There was no fly tower and the pit was simply an area in front of the stage cordoned off for the resident Grosvenor Orchestra and Erard grand piano. However, within a year a new rear extension allowed the stage to be expanded to 50ft wide and 27ft deep and four more dressing-rooms added, but the wings remained narrow. To improve views the stage was raised by 1ft and the back seven rows of stalls were raked. Electric stage lights produced a variety of effects and a stock of scenery included garden, snow and street scenes, palace chamber, library, kitchen, drawing room and prison.

The seats, of varying comfort according to ticket price, and standing room gave a record capacity for Weston of 2,000. Some 200 seats were in narrow side balconies and a deeper rear gallery. The public could use exits at this upper level to enjoy stunning views across the bay from a terrace over the main entrance. A ground-floor tearoom and reading room were complemented by first-floor tearoom and billiard room intended as a high-class club, but without alcoholic drinks. Daytime visitors were charged 2d admission.

Twin front towers containing useful space were off-set by two smaller ones at the back that were simply stairwells giving stage staff direct access to the balconies. A lower basement had a real *Phantom of the Opera* atmosphere about it with boiler room and entrance to a huge settling tank which filled at high tide, mud deposits sank and clear water was pumped through to the baths. A rubber dinghy would be kept in the tank for use by structural engineers inspecting for cracks in the support pillars. Two powerful arc lights on roof standards picked out the pavilion at night. A Post Office Telegraphs superintendent engineer was allowed to use a room for wireless experiments, five years after pioneering transmissions had been conducted in person by Marconi at Knightstone and Brean Down.

Officially it was Knightstone Pavilion but soon acquired the grander title Knightstone Pavilion and Opera House in newspaper advertisements. William Payne, who had run Victoria Hall for the previous ten years, was appointed manager on two guineas a week with free living quarters in a front tower. He had to provide a surety of £100 for the competent performance of his duties.

Both pavilion and pool were opened on Tuesday, May 13, 1902, by Somerset's Lord Lieutenant, the Earl of Cork and Orrey, royalty having declined the offer. After a lavish lunch in the town hall, the Earl, a civic party and visiting mayors were conveyed to Knightstone by Weston's new tramway, also officially launched that day, heavy rain rather spoiling the occasion. The group assembled for a photograph outside the pavilion before the Earl was presented with a handsomely chased gold key to open the building, internally decorated with flags bought for Edward VII's impending coronation, shields and (artificial) flowers. It filled to capacity as the dignitaries took to the stage for speeches. Council chairman Benjamin Heap said

An early view of the small stage, side balconies, barrel-vaulted ceiling and electric chandeliers.

they had met a long-felt need for a public hall and while the cost had been high good results were expected in time.

A grand first-night concert starred eminent soprano Edith Grey-Burnand and principal singers from the Carl Rosa and Italian Opera companies. The *Gazette* noted that while not all the dearer seats were taken, other rows were filled by hundreds wanting to sample the hall's qualities. It praised 'comfortable seats, the blaze of the electric light, softened by silken shades, good ventilation and admirable acoustic properties', but regretted 'an annoying rattle of crockery' from the tearoom that spoiled an otherwise enjoyable evening. Weston had never seen anything quite like the spectacular ball two days later when onlookers packed the gallery as 250 in evening dress or fancy dress, including a Louis XIV, a jester, a toreador, a sunflower, a geisha and a Union Jack, danced to the strains of the Grosvenor orchestra, raising £25 for Weston Hospital.

The pavilion began to fulfil its purpose, the *Western Daily Press* noting a week later that 'a shower of rain about 3pm caused many promenaders to seek shelter and entertainments in the pavilion. Visitors who saw inside for the first time yesterday were very enthusiastic over it.' But the council ran into difficulties from the start. It was unable to book concert parties and bands as summer attractions because they wanted a set fee whatever the box office receipts, which would have broken rules against risk-taking with ratepayers' money. The council was reduced to hiring often lacklustre theatrical companies that would accept sharing terms. A leading firm of concert agents, Baring Brothers of Cheltenham, helped it out of the immediate crisis. It organised high-season entertainment for 65 per cent of takings, the council being responsible for bill-posting and advertising from its 35 per cent share. Some fine bands, including the Scots' Guards, Horse Guards, Blue Viennese, Royal Viennese and White Viennese, and the Berlin Meister Orchestra performed twice daily on selected dates from May to September in 1902 and 1903, admission prices ranging from 6d to two shillings. The Great Western Railway (GWR) ran special excursion trains from Bristol on concert days but despite widespread promotion Baring Brothers lost heavily, their share of ticket income falling well short of musician fees.

This was grist to the mill of a growing lobby critical of the decision to build the pavilion, whose anger erupted every time gloomy annual losses were reported. They accused the council of subsidising what was actually a music hall, and in competition with the private sector, which broke its own golden rule. It had also failed to fully anticipate the impact of the Grand Pier which opened in 1904 with a 2,000-seat theatre and funds to engage the best performers.

Such censure was keenly felt by councillors, who were mostly businessmen or retired businessmen. They considered the pavilion an indispensable attraction and social centre in a maturing resort, planned at a time when a pier seemed illusory, its backers having already secured two delays to their 1893 Act of Parliament. While losses appeared heavy, they included payments to a sinking fund – effectively the mortgage – which would one day end.

Outside of Barings' seasons William Payne did his best to present a varied programme of entertainment within the financial constraints allowed. Silent films had first been shown at the High Street Assembly Rooms and Victoria Hall in the 1890s and they debuted at the pavilion in July 1902 with *Edison's Animated Pictures*. The intention had been to screen footage of Edward VII's coronation but as this was delayed because of his appen-

Knightstone's first orchestra, the Grosvenor.
Left to right: George Tripp (double bass), Harold Smith (violin), Tom Jefferies (flute), Charles T Grinfield (conductor), Bill Jones (cornet), Arthur Tanner (violin) and Gilbert (Bert) Norville (drums). Before the First World War silent films were accompanied on piano by Mr Grinfield or Mr Norville. After the war they were accompanied by the orchestra.

dicitis viewers instead saw a crowd at Windsor reading bulletins about his illness, London street decorations and a review of the troops.

Touring companies presented popular dramas and musical comedies, such as *Florodora*, *San Toy*, *Little Lord Fauntleroy* and *The Casino Girl*, usually over three days. Husband and wife actors Norman V Norman and Beatrice Wilson appeared annually, often in the same productions *Nell Gwyn* and *David Garrick*. There was grand opera, weeks of Shakespeare and boy choirs. Showcase concerts by divas Clara Butt, Emma Albani and Antoinette Sterling could be overbooked and some who paid for seats were infuriated to find they had to stand throughout. 'Psychics' Agnes and Julius Zancig baffled everyone by accurately predicting handbag contents, and the enigmatic entertainer Vulcaris offered £10 if he could not exactly repeat any music played by an audience member. Local illustrated lectures, philharmonic society concerts and children's ballets were slotted between these

Trades, Foods and Industrial Exhibition February 1908

As a means of bringing an infinite variety of goods prominently before the public, such an exhibition as the one being held during this week in the Knightstone Pavilion certainly serves a very useful purpose. An opportunity is afforded of inspecting the various articles exhibited in an interesting and leisurely way, without any invitations to buy.

The many-coloured decorations employed by the various stallholders combined with the crowds of sightseers and purchasers make a very bright and animated scene. There are numerous entertaining sideshows, including Miss Agnes Beckwith's trick swimming, Signor Tano, palmist and character delineator, and Williard's Merry Mannikins. A capital programme of music is rendered daily by Madame Angless' Dutch Ladies' Orchestra.

Of the local stallholders, Mr Cecil Pearson, of Oxford Street, agent for the White Star, CPR Dominion, American, Aberdeen and Leyland lines of steamships, has an interesting and instructive exhibit of the various products of Canada, and literature dealing with the emigration facilities is freely distributed. A feature of this stall is a beautifully executed model of the *Empress of Japan*, a steamer belonging to the CPR line.

Mr HF Dykes makes a speciality of Grip washing tables and Paul's cake flour, a 2lb cake made from a 3½d packet of the latter being on view. The stall of Mr FB Keeping, of the Sweeteries, High Street, has been most tastefully arranged. The expensive variety of sweets and chocolates is charmingly displayed and they certainly look very delicious.

Messrs Norman and Son have on view their well-known blends of tea and coffee, and they provide an additional attraction by offering a cup of either for the modest sum of 1d. The pianos of Messrs HG Millier and Co are beautifully finished, and they have also some exceptionally sweet-toned gramophones, from which selections are played at intervals. In his stall Mr C Veals makes an interesting display of Raleigh cycles.

A comprehensive display of Messrs Fletcher, Russell and Co's gas stoves, etc, is given by Mr JJ Leaver, including a pretty floral radiator, which, although giving out sufficient heat to warm entrance halls, corridors, etc, burns only eight feet of gas per hour. In the small stall there is also an enormous Thermophile gas lamp, of no less than 1,200 candle power, which, however, can be burnt at the remarkably low cost of 1d an hour.

Mr Ernest Widgery, chemist, of West Street, makes a capital show of his tooth powder, whilst Mr H Jelly, of Meadow Street, has a well-arranged display of stationery, post-cards, tobacco, etc. He makes a special feature of his rotary photographic views of Weston, which are being offered for the first time at 1d each.

Mr JS Walker, of Regent Street, shows samples of coal, dog foods, bird seeds, etc. In addition to these exhibits there is a stall for the sale of monogram initials, with ink pad and ink, by the Midland Engraving Company, and a toffee stall by Mr Wantmore (London).

national tour bookings. Visitors to a 1903 trades exhibition witnessed in the accompanying entertainment display a 'flying lady' who inexplicably floated in the air, performing any movement requested by the audience. One early pantomime starred the exotic Mademoiselle Florence who had walked on a globe from London to Brighton and was now cheered by thousands through the streets of Weston as she made her way in similar fashion to the pavilion.

Few Knightstone productions went unaccompanied. The Grosvenor Orchestra under CT Grinfield played before curtain up, during intervals and the National Anthem, if not throughout. Charles Theodore Grinfield was a pianist, composer, author on Handel and cousin of Helen D'Oyly Carte, widow of the Gilbert and Sullivan operas producer. The orchestra ranged in size from a quintette to 12-strong depending on the production but would be stood down when large musical and opera companies brought their own musicians. It performed at the unlikeliest times, accompanying annual Weston and District Chrysanthemum Society exhibitions and playing Irish airs at a Liberal mass meeting on home rule.

Audiences often filled the house, big as it was, and trams waited patiently for shows to end. The *Gazette* was so impressed it declared 'the town will never again revert to its old-time prosy and almost mirthless ways'.

Some must have felt their prophesies of doom about the exposed site were justified when one of the worst storms in Weston's history claimed the life of the pavilion's electrical engineer on the night of Thursday, September 10, 1903. Violent gales whipped up an unusually high tide to swamp the town centre under several feet of water. Eddie Bryant, who had been off duty, struggled out in case he was needed at the hall, but crossing flooded Knightstone Causeway he was unaware in the inky blackness that part of it had been smashed away by buffeting waves. Bryant, the 33-year-old son of a town councillor, was swept out to sea and his body not found for 18 days until it washed up at Pembroke, South Wales, 90 miles away. Meanwhile at the pavilion the audience of 500, who had come to see ventriloquist Lieutenant Walter Cole, thronged to the windows with mounting alarm as water seeped in under the doors. They were cut off, as were another 500 at a swimming gala next door where to everyone's incredulity waves broke over the top of the building, shattering the pool's glass roof. Those who bravely ventured out were lifted off their feet by the strength of the wind and forced back inside. Attempting to leave was suicidal, but more than

Damage to Knightstone Causeway caused by the 1903 storm.

three hours after the storm broke it was finally safe to do so. Repairs to the causeway, the peninsula's wrecked boiler-house and other sea-front damage cost the council nearly £3,000. It was surprised to discover it needed Bristol city council's permission to mend the sea wall, which was under their juris-diction by ancient charter.

The Grand Pier was a serious rival to the pavilion and Payne needed a blockbuster opposite its opening concert by the Milan Orchestra. He presented the first heavyweight film to be shown at Knightstone – award-winning Alfred West's documentary *Our Navy* to stirring musical accompaniment, the gun-firing and skirmishing being loudly applauded. Payne rose to the challenge by booking more shows, tackling a terrible draught when the tabs were open that kept audiences shivering in their overcoats, and arranging for piano interludes to fill very tedious gaps between acts. The famous *Poole's Myriorama* featured at the height of the 1904 season. In this fascinating entertainment, presented by Charles Poole or his brother Joseph, a huge panoramic painting was wound along on rollers while a guide in evening dress explained the unfolding story

The cast of Weston Operatic Society's first production *The Pirates of Penzance* in 1909.

depicted, usually a travelogue or battle scene enlivened with behind-the-scenes flashes and explosions. This time the audience was taken on a stimulating journey from London to Australia and given colourful insights into architecture, customs and natural landscape. When *Poole's* returned during the Great War its graphic scenes of Flanders and Gallipoli were viewed with rapt attention.

The *Western Daily Press* remarked that the 1904 combination of pier and pavilion created a brilliant and successful season that Weston had never seen before, thanks partly to cheap day and half-day train excursions from London. For his praiseworthy efforts Payne was told he could keep the proceeds of programme sales.

The decade continued with drama, concerts, occasional films and Sunday religious services. Thousands flocked to see charismatic (male) evangelist Gipsy Pat Smith preach temperance with almost hypnotic effect for a week in 1905 when the hall could be full to overflowing an hour before the start. A production of *Uncle Tom's Cabin* featured 'real negroes and freed slaves' while another show introduced Weston to six African pygmies who were befriended and showered with gifts by theatregoers. War reporter and future best-selling author Edgar Wallace lectured on *Looking for Trouble*, and *Fabbro's Electric Animated Pictures* showed footage 'specially taken at enormous expense' of Edward VII in Bristol the week before. Variety shows were rare, but for a week *Scottie's Colossal Variety Combine* starred comedians, duettists, dancers, acrobats and a cycling competition. Producer Scott Alexander announced from the stage that he had experienced the hardships of a waif's life and would fund a meal for 200 local children on the Saturday morning, as he claimed to do wherever he performed.

The Liberal Democrat victory in Weston at the 1997 General Election was a jolt to a traditionally Conservative town but was not unprecedented. Weston had long been politically divided: Liberals won the seat in 1923 and its predecessor Wells constituency in 1906 when hustings were first held at the pavilion. Special rail services were laid on from across the constituency so voters could see national speakers. Police were posted on the door during rowdy meetings about home rule and tariff reform, and once reinforcements hid nearby when trouble was expected. The most famous guest speakers were former Prime Minister David Lloyd George and ex-Foreign Secretary Viscount Grey at a National Liberal Federation conference in 1926, which had been postponed because of the General Strike the month before. The Earl of Oxford and Asquith, the former Premier HH Asquith, would have joined them but for ill health. Former Prime Minister Sir Robert Peel's grandson Viscount Peel was one of the best-known Tory grandees to appear, addressing a Conservative mass meeting in February 1914. The most controversial politician to visit was Sir Oswald Mosley, leader of the British Union of Fascists, who turned up with a strong-arm corps of Blackshirts in 1935. As the curtains parted at precisely the 8pm start Mosley strode briskly to centre stage and raised a salute to his supporters, who responded accordingly. On either side of him standard-bearers stood holding the Union flag and the movement's colours throughout his three-hour appearance and on each stage wing a fascist symbol glinted in the footlights. Mosley, whose message essentially was that his party wanted power by constitutional means, was frequently applauded by a full house and heard without disturbance. He dined the next day at the Grand Atlantic Hotel in the respectable company of council leader and magistrate JG Western and the chairman of the Weston branch of the Farmers' Union among others. Earlier that year the Knightstone stage had been taken by William Joyce, Mosley's director of propaganda, who went on to become the Nazi wartime broadcaster nicknamed Lord Haw-Haw.

Back in the first decade of the pavilion, local artist Walter Tucker was paid £250 to transform its bland cream and white interior décor, the result of budget cuts during construction. At Easter 1907, after a six-week closure, audiences marvelled at stencilled festoons, ribbons and wreaths on a background of cream, gold, green, pink and red. The names of composers and leading actors had been listed in gold under two arches.

Weston was inspired to form an Operatic Society of its own after a presentation of *The Mikado* by Wells Operatic Society at the pavilion in 1908. Weston-super-Mare Amateur Operatic Society launched the following year with *The Pirates of Penzance*, a triumph with exceptional talent in the leading parts, notably Leslie J Fursland, an experienced amateur, and Winifred Thomas, a nationally acclaimed soprano and D'Oyly Carte veteran. When Mrs D'Oyly Carte, who gave permission for the three performances, learned from her Weston cousin Charles Grinfield that profits were going to the local hospital, she waived three guineas of her fee. The production was praised for its professional standard and an extra performance was staged by public demand. Annual shows, usually Savoy operas, continued up to the First World War and resumed in 1920 until war intervened again.

Companion amateur group Weston-super-Mare Dramatic Society was founded in the 1880s but re-formed in the last year of the Great War as the public craved entertainment to lift their spirits. The 1918 production, Charles Hawtrey's comedy *The Private Secretary*, was well received and further plays followed almost yearly. Meticulous attention was paid to detail: for a 1936 production of Arnold Ridley's *The Ghost Train* the railway station waiting-room was furnished by the GWR, and two years later the Society borrowed an 1805 copy of *The Times* from that newspaper's archive as a prop in a dramatisation of Jane Austen's *Pride and Prejudice*. The Operatic and Dramatic Societies each sponsored a cot in Weston Hospital from box office receipts.

This local talent often outclassed touring repertory companies, who, despite attracting invariably complimentary press reviews, could struggle to fill seats. To Knightstone's critics that was bad enough but the revelation in 1908 that 21 councillors and departmental heads got free tickets to all shows sparked enormous resentment and became a heated local election issue. Men paraded the streets in sandwich boards that asked 'Why should councillors have free passes to the Knightstone Pavilion and Baths while

"Things have come to a strange pass"—*(Shakespeare).*

Free entry for councillors to the 'white elephant' pavilion
was criticised by the *Weston Gazette* in 1908.

the public have to pay?' A Ratepayers' Protection Association was formed
at a crowded public meeting in the town hall and the council urged to sell
off the pavilion or convert it to profitable use. When an anonymous letter
in the press urged a boycott of the building Payne ceased engaging companies for two weeks in case the call was heeded and their takings were hit.

The council reiterated that the pavilion was a valuable amenity and that
no private owner just out to make money would entertain hospital fund-
raisers. Amateur groups would be priced out and disband. Free passes were
said to be needed in the line of duty: magistrates had granted a licence for
stage plays on condition that two councillors each entered into a £50 bond to
ensure performances complied with the law. But that justified two passes, not
21. Faced with such uproar, passes were restricted to the four members of a
sub-committee directly in charge of the pavilion and to the town surveyor.

Electric Moving Pictures

By the end of the first decade Weston's status symbol had become an embarrassing liability. The pavilion was shut for half of 1909 all told and a heavy burden on the rates. One councillor branded its £1,000 annual losses – though at last decreasing – as 'Monte Carlo madness'. The pavilion was 'a holy of holies, which must not be breathed on or whispered at by way of criticism.' Residents grumbled to the press, one calling it 'a most miserable place of entertainment and it is a thousand pities that such a building should be hanging round the necks of the ratepayers'. Another considered the peninsula 'a dull, dreary place, in itself dispiriting, out of the way and in bad weather simply impossible'.

Miserable perhaps, but it was the best Weston had when the piers were closed and holiday businesses called for more shows in the off-season. The push for a winter visitor season had in fact begun in the previous century, before Orchard Street baker Mr Tottle famously described Weston as 'three months hard labour and nine months starvation'. The town liked to think it could rival anywhere on the south coast as a winter health resort, boasting of its 'champagne air' and sub-tropical plants that flourished outdoors all year as evidence of a mild climate. Abstruse rules prohibited advertising of these attributes from the rates so a voluntary body of local businesses and professional men called the Town Advertising Committee was set up in 1906 with funding from donations to publicise attractions and weather reports in daily newspapers. It shortly became the Town Advertising Association (TAA) which in a few years enjoyed the much-enhanced role of running the beach chairs and major entertainments on behalf of the council, although the pavilion always remained outside its remit.

The council considered laying a maple floor to exploit a roller-skating craze gripping the town, but other rinks opened up and this time it observed the principle of not competing with the private sector. Finally in the drive to fill winter schedules *Electric Moving Pictures*, which had already made a handful of appearances, were introduced on a regular basis in February 1911. The council artfully avoided any accusation of unfair competition – by vetoing plans for Weston's first purpose-built cinema, on the tenuous grounds that the building would be slightly out of street alignment! In an

An early programme cover.

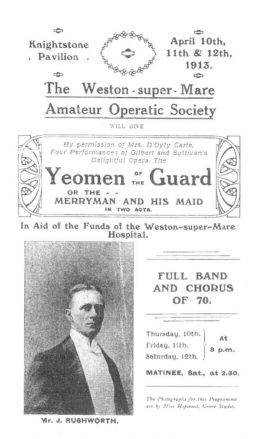

Weston Operatic Society's fifth production *The Yeomen of the Guard* in 1913.
J Rushworth was honorary musical director.

age before effective development control the 700-seat Electric Theatre –
the 'Lec' – was built anyway and at breakneck speed, but Knightstone had
got in first.

The best projection equipment available was installed in an external pod
on the terrace above the main entrance and ten silent shorts at a time shown
to piano accompaniment. The pictures, frequently applauded by an audience
used to live entertainment, were always an eclectic mix and on the first day
ranged from *Wiffles Goes Fishing* and *Fabian Smokes Strong Tobacco* to
Picturesque Scenes in the Loffoden Islands. Soon colour films and *Pathé's
Weekly Animated Gazette* were included and the peerless Mogg's Military

Prize Band played a warm-up on two nights a week. Programmes began at 3pm and 8pm and thousands of handbills were ready for rapid distribution to advertise extra sessions on wet summer mornings.

But after two years of a healthy box office screenings were brought to an abrupt halt, the strict rules on commissioning entertainment again the reason. The Local Government Board auditor harshly rebuked the council for having risked public money on the projection equipment – even though that risk had paid off – and imposed a penalty surcharge equivalent to all the profit it had made on the venture. Only by acquiring the necessary powers in another Weston Parliamentary Act could film shows resume.

Denied of its money-spinner the pavilion once more became a drag on the rates, yet did host major conferences lucrative to the town. Over the years delegations of postal workers, newsagents, booksellers and politicians fed the coffers of local traders and guest houses. Not all events went smoothly: at a 2,000-strong National Union of Teachers convention in 1913 the Lord Chancellor Lord Haldane was persistently barracked by suffragettes who had to be frogmarched from the building.

For now, there were weightier concerns than even votes for women. In 1914 French and Belgian journalists were fêted with a seven-course banquet in a pavilion brightly decorated with national flags. All applauded council chairman Henry Ward's pledge that England would never stand idly by and see French integrity assailed. When war broke out a month later on August 4 it was business as usual with holidaymakers still in town, but an air of deep anxiety soon descended, many rail excursions were cancelled and Knightstone bookings dropped off sharply. The emergency created a small crisis for J Bannister Howard's players worthy of the farce *Oh! I Say!* they were bringing from the Isle of Wight. Their scenery had to be left behind as the railway refused to carry any luggage, forcing them to borrow from another drama company on arrival in Weston.

The pavilion was pressed into war service in a number of ways. At a rousing recruitment meeting Paymaster-General Lord Strachie's revelation that the local MP Captain Sandys had suffered a battlefront bullet wound and lost a lot of blood only hardened the resolve of many to join up, but within days the town was mourning six North Somerset Yeomanry soldiers from Weston, the first of a grim toll throughout the conflict. Billeted troops were entertained by local performers at free weekly smoking concerts, the cigarettes donated by Bristol's Imperial Tobacco Company. Another tranche of troops – which the town actively sought, to boost trade – in 1916 organised their own concerts, drawing on regimental bands and talented singers and comics from the ranks. Wild applause greeted wounded Tommies as they arrived from Ashcombe House, a mansion being used as a 60-bed Red Cross hospital, and their accompanying nurses were playfully accused of seeking more patients as they handed out cigarettes to their charges.

Usually only at Easter and in August and September, with holidaymakers in town, was entertainment provided during the war. In 1915 Robertson Hare, later famous in Aldwych farces and television's *All Gas and Gaiters,* played eponymous retired lawyer Grumpy – at the age of only 23! A production of musical comedy *The Maid of the Mountains* was thrown into chaos through lack of room for its huge amount of scenery. All the second act flats had to be stacked outside, ready to be exchanged during the interval, but in the darkness things got mixed up and act two opened with a confusing mix of first and second act scenery in view. A request by the Grand Pier bandmaster to hire the pavilion for six months from October 1915 at £3 a week was turned down, the council insisting on five guineas a day. No one would pay that much and the premises remained closed for most of the winter, clocking up a hefty loss which it refused to disclose, claiming commercial confidentiality was needed to negotiate the best booking terms. It took the Ratepayers' Protection Association to uncover that there had been a record £2,830 deficit that year, equivalent a century later to £200,000.

In 1916 the local Red Cross was urged to provide 100 more beds and was allowed to use the pavilion as an improvised hospital. But those plans were overturned when the military required the building as a mess for arriving soldiers. The council demanded compensation, physical protection of the property and a pledge to rectify any damage – conditions brusquely rejected by Army top brass who promptly requisitioned it. One can imagine their impatience with such petty officialdom when a war had to be fought. In December military engineers removed all furnishings to the balcony and installed storerooms and kitchens with 32 gas stoves. Even in this altered state the pavilion hosted a Christmas Day Entertainment for Soldiers of humorous songs, piano solos and children's dances – poignantly perhaps the last entertainment some of them would see. Most of the troops left town soon after for their unknown fate and the building was restored to its old self by April 1917. The council lodged a dilapidations claim with the War Office and received £108 10s 9d 'as an act of grace'.

Weston's King of Song

Tenor Harry Arthur Dossor was nicknamed Weston's King of Song because of his many concert appearances. He entertained troops at Knightstone on Christmas Day 1916, and, calling himself Seymour Dossor after his wife's maiden name, conducted or sang at Weston Choral Society concerts in the 1920s when a platform the width of the hall would be set up for 160 singers.

Harry had a brother and son both called Lancelot, the former a baritone concert singer and Weston Operatic Society star with whom he ran jewellers' shop the House of Dossor in High Street. Harry's son was a prize-winning virtuoso pianist, accompanying leading orchestras and becoming professor of piano at Adelaide University. He returned to give a masterly performance at a Knightstone benefit concert for Weston's departing musical director Harry Burgess in 1938.

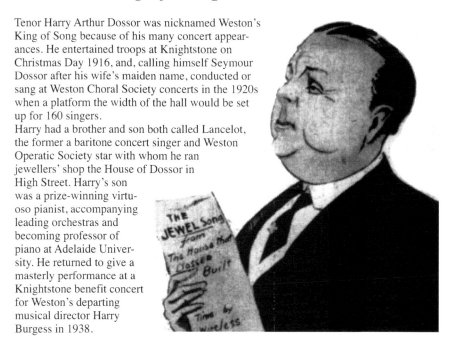

Entertainment for Soldiers of 83rd Provisional Battalion, Knightstone Pavilion, Christmas Day 1916

Pianoforte solo – Private Lloyd
Song – Private Wood
Humorous song – Private Cohen
Dance – Private Hillier
A Carol of Bells (Stanford) – Miss Winifred Hamilton
Humorous Song – Private Scott
Duet – Privates Abraham and Jones
Song – Lieutenant Miller
Dances – Misses A Carter and A Hodges
Humorous song – Sergeant Spencer
Now is the Hour of Enchantment (Goring Thomas) – HA Dossor
Humorous song – Lieutenant Raby
Pianoforte song – Private Lloyd

Song – Private Wood
Til Death (Mascheroni) – HA Dossor
Dance – Miss A Carter
Humorous song – Private Cohen
The Kingsway (Elgar) – Miss Winifred Hamilton
Humorous song – Private Scott
Song – Private Abraham
Dance – Private Hillier
Song – Lieutenant Miller
Humorous song – Sergeant Spencer
Duet – Lieutenants Buckmaster and Raby
Weston-super-Mare Amateur Orchestra (under AH Jennings, conductor AG Dowding)

Church bells rang out, shops closed and crowds gathered in the streets when war ended at 11am on November 11, 1918. Moments later the boom of a gun was heard from the Knightstone direction and everyone rushed there. The muzzle of one of two spiked 40-pounder cannon that featured on thousands of postcards of the pavilion had been stuffed with newspaper, sand and gunpowder and fired in celebration by ironmonger James Leaver without any permission. The crowd was asked to stand back 50 feet while he fired it again. Three days later Mogg's Band and wounded soldiers led a half-mile procession to the pavilion where 2,000 took part in an emotional thanksgiving service. When the Rector, the Rev Prebendary B Norton Thompson, said he wanted to thank, on behalf of others, the wounded men he saw before him he was interrupted by deafening applause from an upstanding audience. The soldiers themselves then struggled to their feet to thank their nurses sitting behind them. As if Weston had not had enough of war, a British Mark IV tank went on permanent display in Alexandra Gardens in recognition of the astonishing £1.5 million raised locally in war savings and as an education to those who had never seen one.

Knightstone returned to normality with the first pantomime in five years and looked forward to a rosier future, for the council now adopted powers obtained in a 1914 Weston Parliamentary Act that permitted financial risk-taking in entertainments by up to a 1d rate. Payne expanded the summer season and at bumper houses holidaymakers let their hair down after four gruelling years of war. But filling the winter diary still proved challenging, constant appeals in the trade press for high-class drama, opera and musical comedies yielding no response, the conflict having taken its toll on the performing arts. The highlights that winter were illustrated lectures by famous polar explorers Sir Ernest Shackleton and Captain Teddy Evans. Ticket queues stretched round the building and there was standing room only to hear Shackleton's gripping account of his Antarctic expedition when his ship *Endurance* was crushed by pack ice and he and a few of the crew undertook a perilous 800-mile mission by lifeboat to reach help.

Now the threat of surcharge had been lifted Payne was able to show films again, this time to orchestral rather than just piano accompaniment. CT Grinfield arranged soundtracks from his own music library – only later did distributors provide musical suggestions – but the orchestra sorely missed its pre-war film accompanist and drummer Bert Norville who had been wounded in battle and was now living in London. The pictures, usually from

Carlton Fredricks' scenery workshop in Langford Road that served his Knightstone pantomimes in the 1920s. Carlton's son Leo is on the left. His other sons James and Wilfred ran their own scenery workshop nearby 30 years later.

the Star Film Company, began in November 1919 with American spy story *The Source*, described by the *Gazette* as 'a really thrilling drama, but like most American films rather far-fetched'. Apart from summer drama, film dominated schedules over the next four years and initially made a welcome profit for the council, which approved 18 Knightstone billboards around town.

Many political, religious and social functions found themselves squeezed out but pantomime was sacrosanct and impresario Carlton Fredricks produced one every year from 1920 until his death in 1926. Fredricks was a larger-than-life character, a humorist, mimic and pantomime dame whose clever speciality was '20 faces under one hat'. He had staged

Carlton Fredricks

his first concert party on Weymouth sands in 1894 before going on tour and finally settled in Weston where he presented shows on the sands and in Grove Park. He leased the Palace Theatre (formerly Victoria Hall) and opened a scenery workshop in Langford Road. His children Della, James, Leo and Wilfred were also gifted performers and James and Wilfred would become Knightstone stage managers. Della's husband Wilfrid Dane wrote, directed and starred in Carlton's pantomimes and once introduced a little flying ballet, attaching a wire to himself so he could soar into the flies. On opening night at the cue 'Fly, birdie, fly' he got ten feet off the ground when the wire snapped and he fell like a stone. Picking himself up he remarked: 'I think we'll cut that out ladies and gentlemen,' and walked off.

The pavilion's run of profitability did not last, thanks to high mainte-nance bills, the need for a new projector and competition from the Regent Picture House and Central Picture House that had opened in 1913 and 1921 respectively. This coincided with a policy of cutting back winter film screenings to three days a week to allow more social functions to be held. Things had not been helped by, of all people, Knightstone committee chairman Barnabas Butter calling most of the live entertainment 'poor, cheap, trashy stuff'. Grand Pier manager Harry Broomfield claimed more than a dozen councillors had never been to the pavilion or on the pier. One, he said, had even boasted of it. A drive for more custom included the introduction of a bookings phone line (the memorable telephone number 75 remained unchanged until 1968 when it became 29075) and a large illuminated sign over the entrance that, in true Broadway fashion, spelled each letter of the word 'Pavilion' consecutively until all were lit, then the sequence was repeated. There were revived calls to lease out the building – a South Wales syndicate was reportedly prepared to offer £2,000 a year – a move that had always been strongly opposed in principle. TAA manager Walter Stray declared that residents had a 'bounden duty' to patronise entertainments in winter as visitors alone could not make them pay – and without entertainments Weston would not attract more winter visitors.

In 1924 the council took the radical step of effectively handing the premises over to Francis Godby and his eight-piece orchestra to arrange concerts, tea dances, Cinderella dances and fancy dress balls on sharing terms, but stopped short of a formal lease. Despite objection from a few religious groups the TAA was allowed to present 25 Sunday concerts on condition they were suitable for the Sabbath – which presumably meant nothing light or comic – and did not clash with church services. They began with the Band of the Black Watch and on one occasion the augmented municipal orchestra and Mogg's Band performed the 1812 Overture with full effects, but the concerts made a loss and the experiment was not repeated.

Losses continued and a desperate shake-up at the town hall placed pavilion management under the wing of surveyor Harold Brown, already responsible for Knightstone baths. Ignoring long-standing political objection he recommended, as one option, letting out the pavilion until the mortgage had been repaid. This was now accepted without demur and in May 1925 a lease was granted to Ernest Stevens, manager of Her Majesty's Theatre, Carlisle, for rising annual rents of £1,000, £1,250 and £1,500, but the council was still left with yearly £900 loan repayments and repair costs. As a strict condition the pavilion had to be kept open all year and available for local functions and amateur theatricals. Stevens installed his son to replace Payne, loyal manager for 23 years, who was transferred to the

Worth's Studios. "H. C. BURGESS and ORCHESTRA" Real Photograph.

The municipal orchestra under HC Burgess performed weekly at the pavilion
in 1924 when it was being run by Francis Godby.

somewhat less-glamorous council housing department.

It was the first year Knightstone hosted the Guy Fawkes Carnival Ball and history was made with the town's first dance broadcast when a Princess Mary Ball featuring the Clifford Essex Band went out on the BBC's Cardiff radio station 5WA. But a repertory company Stevens sent from Carlisle to defy Weston's growing reputation as an actors' grave was taught a lesson in humility. In an interval during Denville Players' first production an actor announced over-confidently from the stage he was sure they would not meet their Waterloo in Weston. Audiences resolutely failed to 'Get the Denville Habit' and the loss-making company left town with its tail between its legs. Stevens also made a loss and ended his tenancy after just one year, raising the uncomfortable question: if seasoned professionals couldn't make the pavilion pay, what hope had the council?

It tried again, dropping the rent to £800, and approved a let from May

Pavilion lessee Gerald Alexander.

1926 to actor-manager Gerald Alexander who ran the Grand Pavilion, Llandrindod Wells. Alexander was no stranger to Knightstone, having presented several touring plays, and now promised West End hits by first-class companies. Staff of many years standing were replaced or made part-time. Shows began 15 minutes later, at 8.15pm, for the benefit of diners, and the orchestra upped sticks to play near the buffet in the second interval to boost refreshment sales.

Entertainers that summer included Bransby Williams, famous for brilliantly impersonating Dickens characters, who 'carried the audience away with the greatness of his art', said the *Gazette*. In a neat touch from the stage, Williams, a London Rotarian, praised Weston Rotary Club as the only branch in England with a boys' holiday home. The audience had been asked to come prepared with questions about historical events, great races and crimes to try to catch out memory man Datas, who appeared on the same bill. Later in the season pioneering wildlife photographer Cherry Kearton gave a running commentary on his jungle film while accompanied by a chimpanzee, said to have the mentality of a five-year-old child, who sat at a table, drank tea, lit and smoked a cigarette and played a mouth-organ.

With quality touring companies thin on the ground, Alexander created his own company called Weston Players with actors hired in London for a season of drama. Despite impressive notices business was poor, not helped by bad weather and a freezing building, the heating system no match for penetrating sea winds. Like Payne before him, Alexander realised that only film-showing was truly profitable and in January 1927 the two projectors were dusted off to screen hits such as *The Mark of Zorro, The Thief of Bagdad, Beau Geste* and *The Gold Rush*. Great War epic *Ypres* was accompanied by an augmented orchestra playing a special arrangement by new resident musical director William Bird.

On a night in March Knightstone suffered another tragedy at the spot where its electrical engineer had drowned 24 years earlier. Musician Jack Cross was knocked down by a taxi on the poorly-lit causeway and died shortly afterwards. Aged just 20 he had led Jack Hylton's Carlton Band at a commercial travellers' dance, a type of event still being held at the pavilion – but for how much longer? Four months later the town opened an elegant ballroom in the convenient sea-front location many had preferred for Knightstone pavilion. The Winter Gardens Pavilion (the Home Secretary vetoed a 'Royal' prefix) had been conceived as a wind-shield for tennis courts, putting green, elongated lily pond and rose garden of Italian design already laid out at the rear. But with smart, grey-uniformed commissionaires, a perfect dancing surface of Australian oak on a unique system of pillars and the savvy TAA in charge, it soon proved itself by poaching the annual Military Ball, Commercial Travellers' Ball and Weston Harriers' Hunt Ball from Knightstone, whose own dance floor, under a revolving ball of 700 mirrors, was deemed 'shabby' by comparison.

A further sign of Weston's progress was the creation the following year of Marine Lake at Glentworth Bay, as envisaged in 1896. Alexander was allowed to run a refreshment stall on Glentworth beach because disruption caused by building the 825ft causeway from Knightstone to Anchor Head had hit income at his pavilion café.

All seats were taken at annual HMV gramophone recitals organised by music shop HG Millier and Co of Handel House, Waterloo Street, which also served as an amateur dramatics box office. The rich tones of Caruso, Beniamino Gigli, Yehudi Menuhin and Gracie Fields filled the hall and 'it did not need much imagination, if one closed one's eyes, to visualise the artists who made the records as being actually on the stage', said the *Gazette*.

A bustling scene on Knightstone Causeway in 1928. The film projector housing can be seen on the terrace above the word 'Pavilion'. At the rear the breakwater is being constructed to create Marine Lake.

Alexander directed some Weston Dramatic Society productions, publicised by on-screen announcements, courtesy of their managements, at the Central and Regent, and now also the new Tivoli cinema, a conversion of the Palace Theatre, itself a victim of cinema competition. The Tivoli, with its own orchestra and lounge, was further serious rivalry and the pavilion did not even open when it launched in 1928 with *Ben Hur* – the epic silent predecessor of the 1959 classic. Alexander persisted with Great War films

A programme for the Red Triangle Players' production of *9.45* in 1928.

The Somme, Verdun, Roses of Picardy, The Emden and *The Flight Commander.* A bid to show *Dawn*, the story of heroic British nurse Edith Cavell executed by the Germans, was initially blocked by the censor because of its anti-German sentiments but the ban was later lifted. Plays were presented in high season and one production, *The Chinese Bungalow,* starred a 21-year-old Rex Harrison. But, as often before, a run of modest success would be jinxed, this time by fire breaking out in the projectionist's box in June 1929. A holidaymaker on the sands raised the alarm after spotting smoke coming from the building, which apart from the box office was closed at the time. A human chain swiftly formed to pass along buckets of water to quell the blaze, which was almost out by the time the fire brigade arrived. There had never been danger of flames spreading as the projection box was made of iron and separated from the auditorium by a thick stone wall, but the projectors could not be saved. Alexander wanted replacements capable of showing talkies, which his competitors were now screening, but the council, which received a £236 18s 9d insurance pay-out, said any upgrade would have to come from his pocket, creating an impasse that halted further film-showing for five years.

It was back to loss-making drama until, seven months later, Knightstone's fortunes were transformed again by fire, but one on a vastly different scale. In January 1930 an inferno fanned by strong winds destroyed the Grand Pier's wooden pavilion, the *Gazette* declaring it one of the most appalling disasters in Weston's history. It had been the town's largest performance hall and its loss left Knightstone in undisputed possession of theatre business.

Bookings were rapidly transferred, notably a three-day gathering of the GWR Social and Educational Union, which while dull-sounding was in fact an extraordinary musical extravaganza. A crowded itinerary included a concert with ten male voice choirs and Swindon's GWR orchestra conducted by famous composer Sir Walford Davies. All of Weston's children got a half-day off school for the arrival by special train of a 16-year-old 'railway queen' to the sort of welcome reserved for royalty. She led a floral carnival procession from the bunting-draped station to Knightstone, a spectacle filmed for cinemas nationwide, and in the flag-lined pavilion a choir of 200 children took part in a broadcast concert. The GWR was an important partner in promoting Weston and that year co-funded with the TAA £1,200 worth of newspaper advertising and railway posters that have become artwork classics. Organisers of regular boxing tournaments, who lost all their equipment in the fire, re-arranged fixtures at Knightstone, and the pier's Sunday bands were re-housed at the Winter Gardens and Knightstone, which secured the prestigious booking of Czech composer Jan Kubelik playing his Stradivarius violin.

In an age when the public didn't flinch at the sight of performing animals, the pavilion – in common with the best theatres – became a 'big top' for circuses and their boxing dogs, waltzing geese, dancing horses and tight-rope-walking monkeys. Boswell's Royal Circus offered £5 to anyone who could keep up with ponies and dogs running on a revolving table, but whether anyone did is not recorded. Another circus arrived early and it was a fascinating sight to see its hulking elephant exercise daily through town. Unfortunately the animal was too big for the pavilion's rear doors so was brought in through the foyer, down the centre gangway and up a ramp to the stage, an unconventional theatrical entrance that nevertheless went well at rehearsal. On opening night, however, things did not go quite to plan. The orchestra struck up *The March of the Gladiators,* the auditorium doors swung open and in strode Minnie the elephant, but when she was half-way up the ramp it snapped, plunging her into the orchestra pit with a great crash of music stands. Minnie tore up the centre aisle trumpeting her indignation, but her keeper was able to pacify her and she submitted quietly to being led outside. Knightstone staff had another close call during magician The Great Carmo's show when a lioness used in his act became loose on stage and they had to run for their lives. Electrician Ernest Toogood recalled: 'We were down the steps and shut in the dressing-room in a moment. The keeper got the lion into the box without any trouble but I'm afraid he had to do it single-handed.' In the same week Mr Toogood had another scary encounter with the animal, which was kept in a cage near the lighting switchboard. One night as he went to turn off the lights after everyone had gone the lioness whipped out a paw behind him. He was cornered and every time he tried to move she struck at him. It was 3.30am before he remembered that above the switchboard was a torch, which he managed to grab and shine in the animal's face, frightening her into withdrawing and allowing him to escape.

A first royal visit to the pavilion was keenly anticipated when George V's son Prince George was invited to address a British Legion national conference on Whit Sunday 1934. In a memorable day for the town he was to take the salute at a sea-front march-past, lay a wreath at Grove Park war memorial then proceed to Knightstone. Every dignitary would be there and more than 100 police officers were drafted in from across the county to control the vast crowds. A pantomime and two balls had raised hospitality funds. But a very public row erupted within the Legion at national level over how the organisation was being run and the Prince felt he could not

Leslie J Fursland was so accomplished a comic opera star the press said he should be listed as one of Weston's attractions. A naturally witty man, he was in his element as Major-General Stanley in *The Pirates of Penzance*, as here in 1934, the uniform hired from a London theatrical costumier. He helped found Weston Operatic Society in 1909 and performed with them for 40 years, often fund-raising for Weston General Hospital where professionally he was secretary.

He entertained troops at Knightstone and in concert parties at army camps in the First World War. But his forte was Savoy operas and once in *The Yeomen of the Guard* he encored a duet so often that his singing partner Frank Bere could stand it no longer. Bere picked him up bodily and with a 'come off, you rascal' raced off stage – an unrehearsed incident which brought the house down.

The two historic cannon were removed for scrap in World War Two.

attend for fear of getting embroiled in the controversy. Unfortunately his decision to withdraw did not reach local organisers in time and the thousands who turned up were unaware he would not be there. There was stunned incredulity and undisguised anger when they were told. The conference went ahead but the pavilion lost the only chance it got of a royal visit. Prince George would redeem himself in the eyes of Westonians eight years later when, as the Duke of Kent, he toured areas of the town heavily bombed in a Luftwaffe raid a fortnight earlier, showing great concern, offering condolences and paying tribute to the indomitable spirit of the population. Within two months he himself was killed in a military air crash in Scotland while on what has been speculated was a secret mission to broker a peace with Germany through a third party.

Despite inheriting pier bookings the 1930s were feast and famine for the pavilion. It could overflow one night for contralto Clara Butt, a picture in ankle-length gown and diamond-studded turban, duetting with baritone husband Kennerley Rumford, then close for a week. The public had gone mad on talkies and few found the pavilion attractive in winter thanks to its impossible heating system. Amateur performers complained they had to wrap up like Eskimos during rehearsals, and some got colds and had to pull out of productions. Alexander struggled on, overcoming the usual temperance lobby objections to open a bar in a converted upstairs office. Given the continuing dearth of quality touring companies, he formed his second drama group since becoming leaseholder – the Gerald Alexander Repertory Company – to present plays now long forgotten, such as *Murder on the Second Floor* and *Paddy the Next Best Thing,* admission charges reduced to cinema prices. Alexander's own dog Thark was cast now and again. For summer variety he resourcefully coaxed down Bristol Hippodrome stars, including 24-stone American xylophonist Teddy Brown who drew a 2,000 capacity crowd with just three days' notice. In an interval the heavyweight musician mopped his neck with a towel and told a pressman he agreed to appear chiefly to show vaudeville was far from dead.

Alexander's greatest coup was booking African-American singer Paul Robeson on Easter Sunday 1934, 'a unique event in the history of Weston-super-Mare entertainment', hailed the press. Robeson had replaced his classical repertoire with folk songs and his selection included traditional Somerset air *Oh no, John! No!* and *David of the White Rock* for those over from Wales. In his trademark deep baritone voice he performed two duets with his piano accompanist Lawrence Brown, a well-known black singer who always travelled with him. He had already sung *Roll de ol' Chariot* but the packed house wouldn't let him go without hearing other favourite spirituals *Old Black Joe*, *Snowball* and, of course, *Ol' Man River.*

But Brown and Robeson's appeal was exceptional. While not dead, 'vaudeville' was on life-support and could only suffer further when the luxury 1,800-seat Odeon opened in 1935. Alexander concluded again that if he could not beat the cinemas he must join them. He offered to raise his rent from £800 to £900 for five years if the council installed sound-film equipment. They declined, so with his own resources he wired the pavilion for sound and launched Knightstone Cinema in June 1934, opening with *I'm No Angel* starring America's biggest box office draw Mae West. This was followed by crowd-pullers *Disraeli, Voltaire, Spitfire, Jane Eyre* and a pre-release of *The Scarlet Empress* with Marlene Dietrich, its first showing in the region. The Odeon's boast of 'purified air' was countered head on with Knightstone's billing as 'the coolest cinema in England' – not a diffi-

cult claim many a frozen theatregoer might have said, except this was high summer when one of the few saving graces of the pavilion's exposed position was that it became a comfortable sanctuary from sweltering heat.

On return now and again to live shows, however, business was as bad as ever. Even principals wooed from the West's best pantomime at Bristol's Prince's Theatre opened to a ghostly auditorium. It was a sign of his predicament that Alexander rather mean-spiritedly demanded extortionate fees for the 1935 and 1936 amateur pantomimes staged in aid of the British Legion. But things did not get that far. In October 1935 there were rumours he was in crisis talks with the council and in no time he gave up the lease and left town without a goodbye. Alexander had battled for nine years to make the

From the *Weston Gazette* in 1938.

pavilion pay and it now reverted to the council which was saddled with the problem again. The *Gazette* declared: 'The town can afford this white elephant no longer. Either it must be reconstructed along modern lines for use as a conference hall or it must go to make room for some new amenity more suited to the position. The latter would probably be the wiser course, for the island is little better than an eyesore.'

Many on the council might have agreed but there wasn't a similarly sized alternative venue available for summer shows. Winter Gardens manager George Latter was moved across to pursue a bold strategy of lavish and heavily promoted live entertainment. He at once stopped feature films, *Death on the Set* appropriately being the last ever shown. With an eye for publicity that was positively Hollywoodian, the cast of a concert party called *Out of the Blue* arrived at Weston's new municipal airport in a blue plane. It was nicely contrived to be the first commercial landing and the council's new publicity and entertainments chief Reginald Gammons was there to capture it on ciné film.

For the 1936 summer the council updated stage lighting and presented a sparkling 12-week revue, a first for the pavilion. Billed as Weston's-super-Fare, *The Show of Shows* starred pantomime favourite Mona Vivian and comedian Will Hay's children Will Hay Junior and Joan. It was an enormous gamble, costing £2,400, but one that paid off: nearly 49,000 saw the four different programmes which grossed more than £4,300. They enjoyed Vivian's clever impressions of Garbo, Ginger Rogers and Mae West and skilled tap dancing. The show's general manager Caspar Middleton was asked to repeat his success the following year.

It was a different story for a Sunday concert when American pianist Charlie Kunz was appalled to discover the grand piano provided was an out-of-tune rattle box. 'Fancy giving me a lump of tin like that to play on! I have never been treated like it before,' he complained later. Two disgusted piano dealers took out a press advert 'desiring to inform the public of this town that neither of them supplied the grand pianoforte which Charlie Kunz used on Sunday night'. Gammons stubbornly insisted there was nothing wrong with it but when the same instrument was used by Lou Preager and his Broadcasting Band the outraged bandmaster threatened to boycott Weston unless things improved.

However, a new piano was not on a list of upgrades approved to keep the momentum going. A ground-floor bar was opened, selling Ansells beers of Birmingham to appeal to the many holidaymakers from that area. Tea was served to patrons at their seats and at times the heating kept on round the clock. News films were screened every afternoon and a revolving stage used for the first time in pantomime *Robinson Crusoe*. Wrington theatrical printers G and M Organ supplied 1,250 free programmes a week in return for a drop advertising curtain, which the *Gazette* thought cheapened the pavilion.

Caspar Middleton's 1937 edition of *The Show of Shows*, a combination of revue, variety and drama that changed weekly over three months, was the most expensive seasonal show ever staged in the town. It was another winner and a special midnight performance was broadcast by the BBC to the Empire. Despite good weather that kept holidaymakers outdoors takings

A variety show in September 1938.

were down by only £200 on the year before. At the final curtain on the last night, attendants trooped down the gangway with trays of presents for the multi-talented cast. But Sunday concerts were plagued again, this time with such a bureaucratic muddle that the booked bandleaders Joe Loss and Ambrose stayed away in protest. In desperation the council turned to Middleton, having earlier refused his offer to organise them. He responded with gusto, laying on a series of *Shilling Sunday Popular Concerts*, including a celebrity edition with comedian and singer George Robey.

The Show of Shows' success was a fitting backdrop to Weston's incorporation as a borough by royal appointment, celebrated with a Knightstone concert with Al Lever's orchestra. Incorporation had been a dividing issue for years, with many questioning the cost and benefits. As early as 1923 a mass meeting at the pavilion had narrowly voted in favour of the enhanced status over the alternative of a three-year delay – a hollow victory given the time the town would have to wait. For the first time Weston had a mayor, quarry owner Henry Butt, who wore a grey homburg hat, smoked Churchillian cigars and rode around in his own chauffeur-driven white Rolls-Royce Phantom limousine. He was a rough diamond but had a heart of gold and raised thousands of pounds for the local hospital. Despite the prestige of office he was never prouder than at his daughter's wedding, for which he held a spectacular ball for 400 guests at Knightstone in 1909.

No one let the council run away with the idea that the pavilion's tentative recovery had settled its future. There were calls for a modern replacement nearer the town centre, Middleton himself suggesting a 1,200-seater in Grove Park. The headmaster of Weston County School TE Lindfield's criticism was the most graphic. Presenting shows at the pavilion, he said, was like 'offering dinner to guests and asking them to eat it out of a dog's saucer. It is not a theatre, was never intended to be a theatre and is unsuitable as a theatre.'

He might have been astonished at how things would turn out.

The Three Musketeers

Most holidaymakers had packed their suitcases and left town by the time *The Summer Revellers* concert party breezed into Knightstone. It was a season late, arriving in the autumn shadow of *The Show of Shows*, but was a scintillating week of song, comedy and dance produced by George Hay and Gordon Lane who would soon take over the pavilion and mastermind its most triumphant era. No one knew that yet – for now, they were en route from a successful run at St Anne's-on-Sea to a four-month tour of South Africa.

Lane was a local man, a respected impresario, Weston Dramatic Society producer and chairman of the TAA entertainments committee. With Hay he staged simultaneous summer shows at seaside resorts and somehow also found time to run the Crosby Hall Hotel in Royal Crescent. Hay, a graduate of the Royal Academy of Music and former chorus master of the Old Vic opera, was an effortlessly fluent composer, pianist and baritone singer. Together their formidable talents bred only the highest of standards. Sydney Barnes, a dancer and light comedian star of *The Summer Revellers*, would make a distinctive mark on Knightstone during the Hay-Lane tenure.

Successful as the 1937 summer had been Knightstone made a loss for the year and Gammons, who had predicted otherwise, left his job. His dual role of entertainments and publicity was split, creating an accommodation crisis, and dynamic new publicity manager Edward Turner discovered his office was a cramped garret at the pavilion. Caspar Middleton temporarily advised on entertainments and recommended new stage curtains and proscenium decorations and a heating system overhaul. In April 1938 Turner relocated to the town hall and his Knightstone room became an air-raid precautions office.

The first hint of the transformational changes at the pavilion came when a successful businessman and independent town councillor offered to take it over. George Bosley was foremost a caterer who ran the sea-front Melrose Café and had turned the Winter Gardens Café Continental into a money-spinner for the council. He was also an established entertainer, having presented teenage crooner Reg Varney and other cabaret acts at the Melrose, and, as a member of the exclusive Inner Magic Circle, amazed and baffled

Victor Dimoline as Idle Jack, Monty Price as Greta the Goose and Wilfred Roe in the title role of *Mother Goose*, the British Legion pantomime in 1939. Roe was a towering figure in Weston amateur dramatics for over 40 years, preferring dame roles. He produced many pantomimes, chaired Weston Dramatic Society and was a life member of Weston Operatic Society. It was a double life – Conservative councillor and dentist by day and perhaps ageing ballerina singing *She's One of the Back-Row Girls* by night.

everyone with quite exceptional skill in Knightstone pantomimes. Bosley promised shows far superior to anything Weston had seen and hoped to open with Gracie Fields.

However, he was up against new entertainments manager William Jackson who wanted council venues under his control so he could ensure they complemented each other. Frank Fortescue, whose repertory company was currently playing to thin audiences, bluntly warned that the pavilion had a bad name in the profession but Jackson believed that with recent auditorium and stage improvements things were looking up. And live shows, nearly killed off by the talkies, were making a comeback, as Bristol Hippodrome's imminent return from cinema to theatre proved. Jackson envisaged a full Knightstone winter programme of variety, revues, musical comedy and plays, accompanied by the municipal orchestra. True, its location was a real handicap but his solution was free (council-funded) bus travel for those with booked theatre tickets or a dedicated taxi fleet to ferry patrons door-to-door. He might not make a winter profit but he could avert a loss.

At first, on the chairman's casting vote, Mr Jackson's plans were rejected by the council who favoured leasing out, even a Labour man sighing they had 'tried Knightstone Pavilion drunk and tried it sober'. That decision was reversed after an outcry in the press which, contrary to their previous stance, now argued that if the pavilion really could succeed it should be the ratepayers who reaped the benefit.

But events were about to overtake Mr Jackson, starting with a shameful episode in Weston's entertainments history. For years concerts by the municipal orchestra under HC Burgess had delighted tens of thousands of holidaymakers, so there was widespread anger when cuts to its £3,000 budget were planned. In July 1938 Harry Burgess resigned, accusing the council of failing to consult him on key issues such as the engagement of singers and admission price rises. In extraordinary scenes Weston had rarely seen before, thousands packed protest rallies demanding the council rescind its decision to accept his resignation. But Burgess's mind was made up and at a farewell concert at Knightstone he was presented with a handsome testimonial cheque and everyone sang *For he's a Jolly Good Fellow*.

With Burgess gone, followed by several of his loyal musicians who defected in disgust to the new Bristol Hippodrome orchestra, Jackson's plan for a Knightstone winter orchestra was unrealistic. Meanwhile Hay and Lane had returned with *The Summer Revellers* now at the 300-seat Grove Park Pavilion – an unusual glass-roofed, open-sided structure – where even the most glacial of Weston's high society rolled laughing in the aisles at the sensational civic première. Its 17-week run played to consistently full houses, overshadowing a Knightstone revue called *Out of the Hat*, Caspar Middleton's uncharacteristically disappointing third-year offering. His intensive re-writing, a broadcast night and even an auditorium make-over couldn't save it. Knightstone plunged deeper into the red, wiping out all the profit at Grove Park where receipts had trebled.

A troupe of Mavdor dancers in *Mother Goose* in 1939. Mavdor Dancers and Mavdor Babes, trained by sisters Mavis and Doreen James at their Mavdor School of Dancing, featured in Knightstone pantomimes for nearly 40 years.

The council had had enough and agreed to re-let Knightstone. When George Hay, Gordon Lane and George Bosley joined forces to submit a bid they were the obvious choice among nine tenderers. With Hay and Lane's artistic flair and Bosley's financial muscle it was a dream ticket. The *Gazette* remarked: 'These three are in a position to offer us entertainment of a calibre almost unknown to Weston. It is a pity they have not a modern theatre for the purpose, but I'll warrant they'll make very good use of Knightstone.' Their new company, Knightstone Theatre Ltd, which Lane chaired, was granted a three-year lease from April 1939 at £800-a-year rent, with an option to renew. The company name reflected the official new title: no longer Knightstone Pavilion; now Knightstone Theatre.

The directors paid four times the £210 average salary for one of Britain's leading impresarios to manage the theatre. Paul Murray had worked his way up the Stoll organisation to become London Coliseum's booking manager and helped open Bristol's Bedminster Hippodrome. In management on his own he had staged a string of hit shows starring Jack Buchanan, Gertrude Lawrence, Jack Hulbert and Cicely Courtneidge. He was now handed enormous power to guide policy, engage artistes and run the theatre. Money would be no object.

Knightstone suddenly acquired an indefinable, almost magical formula of success that had eluded it for so long. New carpets and wing curtains gave the auditorium a luxurious feel; employees won a generous pay rise – but strictly in return for courteous and willing service; and bar staff were issued with smart new uniforms. A direct phone line linked box office with ticket agent HG Millier's music shop and special bus services were arranged for before and after performances. But the biggest revolution was on stage. The standard would now bear comparison with anywhere in the country – even the West End.

Over the 1939 Easter weekend Opposition leader Clement Attlee was among Co-operative Party delegates amused to be greeted by a large banner strung over the theatre entrance announcing *Crazy Days*. This was not a reference to their conference but to the lessees' superb launch production in the coming week. A top-grade comedy, it starred the famous Lupino family and Gretchen Franklin among 30 artistes, with music by Billy Mayerl, who conducted the orchestra. The show was slick, clean and packed with laughs, and audiences roared their approval. It was a most impressive start.

That was followed by a brilliant new Weston Repertory Company, created from scratch by Murray who handpicked the best talent on trips to London, paying well over the odds for a provincial theatre. They opened to a crowded VIP house with *George and Margaret*, a light domestic, if risqué, comedy with the suggestion of a couple's son seen in the maid's bedroom. Critics went wild about the standard of drama presented week after week, claiming it emulated anything on offer elsewhere, even Liverpool, the home of repertory excellence. Occasionally the cheque book came out to tempt stars Sarah Churchill, Phyllis Neilson-Terry, Irene Vanbrugh and Richard Goolden into productions. But they could be eclipsed by the high-calibre

George Hay (early picture)

Gordon Lane

George Bosley (early picture)

Sydney Barnes

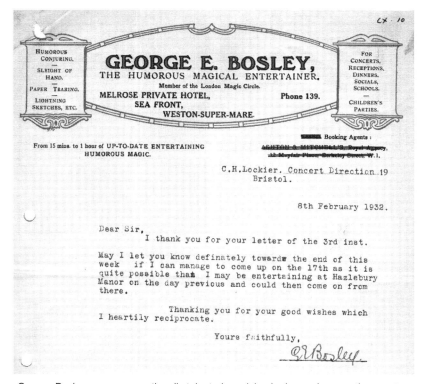

George Bosley was an exceptionally talented magician in demand across the country.

repertory actors such as Constance Chapman, who became a prolific radio and television performer, Christine Bennett, Ann Wrigg and Jean Tait. Playgoers were treated to a broad range of drama, from light comedies *Hay Fever* and *The Importance of Being Earnest* to the weighty *Saint Joan* and *The Shining Hour*. The response was overwhelming and extra seats were installed on balcony daises in already the country's largest repertory theatre. Season tickets rapidly disappeared and one thrilled fan offered the management £200 to maintain the standard but was politely refused as they did not need money in that way. It was the perfect answer to councillors who had openly predicted the tenants 'will wish they'd never seen the place'.

In the glorious summer before the outbreak of war the fare turned to twice-nightly variety and every show sold out. The town was besieged with holidaymakers and queues stretched the length of Knightstone Causeway as tickets went on sale for Billy Bennett, Stanley Holloway, Evelyn Laye and

The Summer Revellers, Weston-super-Mare, 1938.

The Summer Revellers appeared at Knightstone in 1937 and Grove Park
Pavilion the year after. Sydney Barnes is pictured centre.

Henry Hall. Gracie Fields would have appeared but for illness. Performers
at one Sunday concert had to sleep in cars on the sands or under beach
chalets as no rooms were available anywhere in town. When in London
Murray checked out the Café de Paris for original talent and booked their

resident bandleader Ken 'Snakehips' Johnson and his West Indian Orchestra for a night – a year before Johnson was tragically killed when a bomb scored a direct hit on the Café.

Everyone of course knew war was coming and was determined to enjoy themselves before it did. In September 1938 Prime Minister Neville Chamberlain's now-famous 'gasmask' speech had been relayed to Knightstone with chilling effect and was solemnly followed by the orchestra playing *Abide with Me* and the National Anthem, both of which the audience sang standing. The new RAF Locking geared up for an influx of hundreds of airmen.

The theatre closed on the declaration of war, but for only a week prior to an autumn repertory season arranged as a morale-booster. Hay and Lane took *The Summer Revellers* back to Grove Park Pavilion, a venue they also applied to run but the request never left the council in-tray. But for the war they might have been even more ambitious – several times they seriously considered building a town centre theatre with modern facilities that Knightstone lacked. All they could do for now was upgrade Knightstone, steadily resembling a proper theatre with a fully-stocked costume department in the front left-hand tower and a refurbished café with daytime live music where customers could mingle with the stars. The intention was to keep the café open until midnight in summer. However, a planned fly tower and revolving stage never materialised.

In June 1940 the Winter Gardens Pavilion was requisitioned, leading the council (too hastily, some said) to disband the municipal orchestra which had survived under Mozart Allan after Harry Burgess's departure. The two historic cannon at Knightstone were ordered to be removed for scrap, and it was the end, too, for financial reasons, of the eccentric Weston, Clevedon and Portishead Light Railway, affectionately known as the WC & P. 'Where will local comedians find their jokes now?' wondered the *Gazette*.

After bombs fell in surrounding villages in mid-July the theatre was closed for a sober assessment of the position. Knightstone's directors had to admit the peninsula stood out like a sore thumb and would make an easy target. The theatre was nevertheless re-opened but when more bombing in September killed seven people and injured 50 in Banwell and Locking the doors shut indefinitely, apart from a lecture by author and historian Bernard Newman on The Nazi War Machine and a municipal orchestra benefit concert.

At the end of September it was announced the building would become

Chris Charsley

When Chris Charsley took up his pen to write pantomimes for the Knightstone stage it was but the latest facet of the life of a remarkable, multi-talented man. That they were great successes would have come as no surprise to anyone aware of his extraordinary past.

Born in Leicester in 1864 he joined Birmingham Police, rising to the rank of hackney carriage department inspector before becoming one of the youngest-ever Chief Constables at the age of 34, for Coventry. While in Birmingham he had played for the city's football team Small Heath as an amateur, displaying outstanding skill that got him capped as England goalkeeper in their 6-1 victory against Ireland in 1893.

Mr. C. C. Charsley, Chief Constable, Coventry.

The Midlands were bombed by Zeppelins in the First World War and Mr Charsley retired early from the police to move his family to the presumed safety of Weston-super-Mare, taking with him a salvaged fragment of the first airship to be shot down over Britain, which he used as an inkwell. In Weston he was recruited by MI5 and tasked with investigating Bolshevik infiltrators into the British trade union movement, his diary noting that one or two were known to carry firearms.

He joined Weston council, his integrity and wise counsel seeing him promoted to deputy mayor, and only his Roman Catholicism unofficially barred him from the office of mayor itself. Prior to the Second World War Mr Charsley countered widespread scepticism with tact and diplomacy to establish an efficient civil defence force for the town made up entirely of volunteers. This served Weston well during horrific Luftwaffe attacks, he tirelessly overseeing operations night and day as Somerset sub-controller in charge of the 140 square mile district until his death in early 1945. Later there was an enormous groundswell of indignation that he had never been honoured for his service to the town and his previous distinguished career.

While in the police Mr Charsley developed a keen interest in amateur dramatics, which he pursued in Weston, scripting and producing amateur pantomimes, first at Whitecross Hall, then Knightstone, that earned glowing reviews. *The Sleeping Beauty* in 1939 was praised by a critic as 'one of the slickest, funniest and most picturesque shows I have seen on any amateur stage'. He composed the music too, having taught himself to play the piano and flute. Mr Charsley wrote books about goal-keeping and for children and lengthy stories that were published in local newspapers. He dragooned his son Don onto the stage but didn't live to see him flourish as a comedy star in British Legion pantomimes, several of which he also produced. Chris is pictured (above) in an amateur production.

A bill poster from May 1942.

a clothing factory for the rest of the war, the censor judiciously banning mention that the clothing in question was battledress. The transformation was swift: after the benefit concert workmen took just two days to move all furniture and fittings into store and install a bank of sewing machines for 200 female staff. The theatre had not been requisitioned but sub-let – with council permission – to a company evacuated from London, a decision attacked by the press who complained the flag of entertainment was being lowered too quickly.

George Hay, who had staged shows overseas for First World War troops, now at 54 went off with ENSA to serve his country again. Mr Murray accepted a managerial offer from NAAFI and would not return, Gordon Lane produced a long-running show at Rozel Bandstand and George Bosley remained in catering and on the council, chairing its Publicity and Public

Relations committee.

The theatre escaped damage in the first major blitz on Weston in January 1941 when 34 were killed and Grove Park Pavilion was completely destroyed, a section of park railing becoming embedded high in a tree for 70 years as a lasting reminder. To lift spirits, a downed Messerschmitt 109 was displayed at the Winter Gardens tennis courts, some of the 6d admission going to an air-raid distress fund.

Another devastating attack over two nights in June 1942 put Weston in the august company of Bath, Canterbury and York as targets of the infamous Baedeker raids on cultural centres, carried out in reprisal for British bombing of the ancient ports of Lubeck and Rostock. It was the worst bombardment on Weston, leaving 100 dead and 400 injured, some machine-gunned from low level as they fled burning homes. The Tivoli cinema was among the many buildings destroyed, but once again Knightstone was spared. On Home Guard duty outside their Langford Road drill hall was an 18-year-old budding actor who would soon appear at Knightstone en route to film stardom. Tony Britton recalled: 'A mate of mine had joined as well and that night we were both on duty with our rifles – probably without ammunition as I shouldn't think they trusted us with any. We heard the sound of an aeroplane in the distance and it came nearer and nearer. It was probably no more than 300 feet up because one could see the pilot – it was a very bright night. Suddenly we saw little white flashes coming out from the front of it. I said "Bloody hell, come on, over the wall". Then the raiding party appeared and started dropping fire bombs all over town. They landed in the streets all around us and smashed through roofs, landing on people's beds, so we spent most of the night going into houses getting these incendiaries out and making sure the people got out safely. Meantime my mother was at home in Milton wondering what the hell was going on. I think she must have been so terrified. I couldn't get back there until the morning.' Why Weston was a Baedeker target, chosen from travel guides published by the German family of that name, is unknown, as the only description of it in the 1937 edition is 'a popular watering-place'. Other reasons have been given for the raid.

Four months earlier an advertisement placed in *The Stage* trade newspaper by Knightstone's directors seeking contact with former members of Weston Repertory Company sent rumours buzzing round town that the theatre might not be closed for the duration after all. Confirmation was issued to the press that it would indeed re-open that Easter, and so began in earnest its use as a number one circuit variety house – quite a coup for a town of just 41,000 residents.

Children's ecstatic laughter as football-jerseyed dogs nosed balloons around the Knightstone stage and attacked the referee's trousers in the madcap first show was welcome tonic for a war-weary Weston. George Hay had returned to conduct a new-look Twentieth Century Variety Orchestra which was at work even during intervals with melodies from popular musicals. For a few hours a beleaguered public could escape bleak reality and enjoy a sparkling, luxuriously dressed show like *Victory Vanities* with comedian Frank O'Brian, which one critic considered an extraordinary achievement given the times. Theatregoers weren't allowed to forget Britain's war partners with productions such as *Inter-Allied Variety Week* that featured Captain Strelsky and his fast and furious Russian Cossack Band in silk shirts and fleece hats, or *Hello, America* – though goodness knows what the GIs who first arrived in the country that year made of Lancashire comedian Nor Kiddie and sand dancers Wilson, Keppel and Betty who topped the bill. George Formby's brother Frank appeared in musical burlesque *Lady, Meet the Navy* with film star Leslie Fuller, who had cut his teeth as a comedian in a Madeira Cove concert party in 1914.

The Baedeker raid coincided with a revue inaptly named *Nights of Gladness* and little did its first audience realise that two of the company had been dug out of a bombed house earlier in the day by the assistant stage manager or that chief comic Cyril Dowler was just out of hospital after a raid on York. In true stage fashion the show went on with boisterous fun that defied the carnage outside.

War service made it impossible to re-form Weston Repertory Company and the autumn and winter seasons were instead snapped up by actor-manager Bernard Benson. Audiences were asked to bring gramophone records for intervals. Benson was short of an actor for comedy *Quiet Wedding* and took on Tony Britton, by now a promising Weston Dramatic Society newcomer. Tony recalled: 'For a week, I think Benson gave me £2 10s. He needed an older actor but they had all been called up. He asked the amateur companies and got me, terrified and without any stagecraft. But the company were patient and kind and I remembered a few things I learnt, and recalled about five years later when I was demobbed from the Royal Artillery and trying to find out how to get a job in the theatre.'

Wilfred Fredricks

James Fredricks senior

After war service as a gunnery lieutenant Tony returned to Weston amateur dramatics and made one more appearance at Knightstone – but not on stage. As a 23-year-old eligible bachelor he was chosen to escort a 19-year-old Shirley Temple lookalike on a night out organised by the Odeon to promote the Cary Grant-Shirley Temple film *Bachelor Knight*. At the wheel of a Mercedes-Benz roadster Tony drove her to a hotel for cocktails and dinner, followed by an appearance on the Odeon stage. Then they were off to see variety show *Ladies in Review* at Knightstone before ending the night at a Winter Gardens dance. A well-connected drama critic found Tony small parts on the professional stage and later a job as an assistant stage manager in Manchester. That set him on the path to film fame, including roles in *Operation Amsterdam* and *The Day of the Jackal*, and television series *The Nearly Man*, for which he won a best actor award.

All backdrops for Benson's seasons were made by Carlton Fredricks' son James, Knightstone's stage manager, who later ran a studio in Langford Road producing high-quality scenery for theatres nationwide. Flax cloths 36ft long and 24ft high were decorated with aniline dye rather than paint so they could be folded for transportation. At Knightstone, because there was no fly tower, they were rolled lengthways on stage, attached to a lowered baton and hoisted deadweight on pulleys – a strenuous ordeal for two flymen. Smaller cloths could be folded and 'tumbled' down.

James' son, also James, recalled: 'During the war dad worked driving a petrol lorry and as a stage manager at Knightstone. He kept the job at the theatre until his younger brother Wilfred was demobbed from the Army and took over as stage manager. Dad was able to start his scenery business because a repertory company that had been performing for the season wanted to finish by doing a musical. They asked dad to teach them to dance and I believe he produced the show for them as well. It was evidently a great success and they were so pleased with the result that when the final curtain came down they gave him £100. Considering that his wage at the time was about £3, this represented a fortune. He came home and threw the bank notes on the bed. Mum and I thought he must have robbed a bank or something. He took us on a holiday to Blackpool and Morecambe and with the remainder of the money he bought material to start his scenery business. He painted the first few cloths in my bedroom before renting the back of Clifford Pitman's warehouse. Wilfred continued working at Knightstone until dad had built the business and he eventually came in and managed the firm.

'I would often go to Knightstone as a small boy. George Hay and his friend Sydney Barnes – who must have been one of the funniest pantomime dames ever, although I am told my grandfather Carlton was brilliant in that role as well – were always very kind to me.'

A 9pm bus curfew and petrol rationing that forced many taxis off the road could have hit Knightstone severely during the blackout, especially as Weston had many elderly and infirm residents, so performances were brought forward to start at 6.30pm. Rationing also affected the licensed bar, which opened only when supplies permitted, but the café was well stocked and a substantial meal could be had for a shilling. Snacks were available in the foyer or from usherettes, whose lilac uniforms – with hats – were made by Gordon Lane's wife Kathleen in the wartime spirit of improvisation.

After six months of Benson's plays, Christine Bennett from the old Weston Repertory Company returned to produce comedy *Love in the Mist,* in which she starred with 23-year-old Donald Pleasence, the future film star on leave from the forces, and his wife Miriam Raymond. Most of the cast had been engaged in war work and not always able to rehearse together, but acted outstandingly, Pleasence performing 'with complete assurance and

I, the Lord Chamberlain of The King's Household for the time being, do by virtue of my Office and in pursuance of powers given to me by the Act of Parliament for regulating Theatres, 6 & 7 Victoria, Cap 68, Section 12 Allow the Performance of a new Stage Play, of which a copy has been submitted to me by you, being a pantomime in 4 Acts, entitled " The Sleeping Beauty " with the exception of all Words and Passages which are specified in the endorsement of this Licence and without any further variations whatsoever

Given under my hand this 25th day of January 1939.

Clarendon

Lord Chamberlain

Until 1968 all stage productions had to be vetted by the Lord Chamberlain, who by Victorian statute was charged with upholding theatrical standards of good manners, decorum and public peace. A licence was issued stipulating that there should be no variation to the approved dialogue whatsoever. Here permission for amateur pantomime *The Sleeping Beauty* was issued just eight days before the production was due to begin at Knightstone in February 1939. The reverse of the certificate drew attention to regulations that had to be strictly observed. 'Any change of title must be submitted for the Lord Chamberlain's approval. No profanity or impropriety of language to be permitted on the stage. No indecency of dress, dance or gesture to be permitted on the stage. No objectionable personalities to be permitted on the stage, nor anything calculated to produce riot or breach of the peace. No offensive representations of living persons to be permitted on the stage.' The producers of Weston's British Legion pantomimes, notorious for ad-libs and ridicule of local politicians, must have been confident these rules were unlikely to be rigidly enforced.

Pantomimes usually featured speciality acts. In British Legion pantomime *Robinson Crusoe* in 1947 dance tutor Judy Alexander and Stanley Bond demonstrated 'how everyone would like to be able to dance, but very few can,' said a press review.

rare finesse', said a review.

It was a prelude to an even better variety season than the year before. In 1942 big stars saw Weston as a gamble and wanted financial guarantees but after consistently large houses word spread that it was a first-class date, making it easier to book the likes of Sandy Powell, Beryl Reid and Issy

Bonn. Gordon Lane, now general manager as well as director, could even afford to be choosy, signing no contract until he was satisfied with the support acts. He was also able to stipulate standards of propriety. Broad humour was one thing, smut quite another, even if it got past the Lord Chamberlain. Notices in every dressing-room warned against material that could offend family audiences, and one star was told the curtain would be rung down on him if he kept defying an order to cut a certain gag. After that experience Lane demanded to see comedians' scripts in advance and one Monday morning made three artistes change their entire material before first house. He was no puritan but was acutely aware of the temperament of a very conservative town and backed a *Gazette* campaign to clean up the stage. This gained national notoriety and in a backlash a few acts elsewhere irreverently mocked 'Weston – the holy city', while an indignant Issy Bonn launched an audacious, if courageous, broadside from the Knightstone stage on what he saw as an attack on the whole profession.

Cultural standards were maintained too with the first-ever ballet visit. The Ballet Rambert, sponsored by wartime creation CEMA, the Council for the Encouragement of Music and Arts, appeared twice in two months with Sally Gilmour, Sara Luzita and Elisabeth Schooling among the performers of a series of scenes rather than complete ballets. Shortly after the war the newly formed Bristol Old Vic company presented JB Priestley's latest play *Jenny Villiers*, which Priestley himself considered 'a piece of damned good luck' for Weston and impossible without support from CEMA's successor, the Arts Council of Great Britain. The production, which included a future Dr Who, Patrick Troughton, and a future comedy film star, Kenneth Connor, was 'the most outstanding event in Weston's theatrical history', eulogized the *Gazette* critic, who had never seen Knightstone's stage used to better effect. Scenes were changed in momentary blackouts and spotlight pinpointing gave reality to dream sequences. The Oldmixon Players were paid a rare tribute when playwright Ben Travers turned up on the last night of his farce *Rookery Nook*. Speaking from the stage afterwards he declared it the best presentation of the play he had seen.

As war drew to a close Lane treated Weston to a galaxy of radio stars who had kept up morale on the home front, including *Happidrome's* Harry Korris (Mr Lovejoy) and Robbie Vincent (Enoch), The Two Leslies and Douglas Byng. Gracie Fields' brother Tommy topped the bill in the knock-about *We'll Meet Again,* and the all-male ex-servicemen's *We Were in the*

Forces, whose posters promised 'Lovely Ladies in Skirts', played to full houses. On VE Day pantomime dame Clarkson Rose's famous revue *Twinkle* was in town, enjoying its 25th season on the road. For a special victory edition the theatre was temporarily floodlit, as were the Winter Gardens Pavilion, cinemas and town hall. And when Dorothy Summers and the gang from *It's That Man Again* starred in a show named after her character Mrs Mopp's catchphrase 'Can I Do You Now, Sir?', Knightstone's directors had to spend their time directing huge box office queues and traffic that had jammed the causeway. On the first night there were gales of laughter from an audience of servicemen and women home on leave at the bashful embarrassment of a hefty six-foot sergeant induced to assist Mrs Mopp, but he was rewarded with a kiss on both cheeks from her. Stand-down parades were held on stage by the 8th (Weston) Battalion of Somerset Home Guard and Weston-super-Mare and District Civil Defence Unit who had done such sterling work in six years of conflict.

The war was over but a tradition that had begun in those dark days would come to define the management's talent and originality. Knightstone had long hosted amateur and imported pantomimes but in 1944 Hay and Lane created a brilliant version of the genre. *Babes in the Wood,* written by comedian David Graves who had been associated with both men since the days of *The Summer Revellers*, contained all the elements of a big-city equivalent, with speciality acts, London ballet troupe and 12 elaborate scenes by James Fredricks. It was stunningly dressed, beautifully choreographed and painstakingly rehearsed. In one clever routine the Passmore Brothers danced with dummies, and a novelty circus turn included performing bears and a horse that did tricks and gave rides down the aisle. In a movingly patriotic set piece, a chorus of 20 girls formed an inverted victory-V by sitting on each other's knees while Robin Hood sang the stirring *Song of Liberty* to Elgar's fourth *Pomp and Circumstance* march. It was all rather magical to Weston's children but only the first in a succession of house pantomimes whose fame would spread far and wide during the golden era of Hay, Lane and Bosley – now being affectionately dubbed by the press as The Three Musketeers.

Variety Heyday

After completing their down-bill act, singers Ted and Barbara Andrews placed an upturned tub behind the microphone and made an announcement. It was their young daughter's birthday and they had brought her with them. With that, freckle-faced Julie skipped on from the wings in light frilly frock, stepped onto the tub and enchanted the audience with the song *Come to the Fair* in exquisite coloratura soprano voice. It was clear the talented youngster was headed for stardom and Julie Andrews would at the age of 12 become the youngest-ever solo act at a Royal Variety show. Within 20 years she had scooped an Academy Award for her debut film performance in *Mary Poppins* and a Golden Globe for *The Sound of Music*.

Julie's parents had needed George Hay's permission for her unbilled appearance – one of several over two years in the seaside resorts where they performed. She recalled: 'I had to stand on a beer crate to reach the microphone to sing my solo. My mother played the piano, my stepfather sang, and once in a while I joined him in a duet. It must have been ghastly but it seemed to go down all right. Some of the theatre managers wouldn't take a chance on a rather ugly ten-year-old child. They thought my parents were quite out of their minds. But the ones that did take a chance were very nice.'

It was a classic moment from Knightstone's twice-nightly variety heyday in the late 1940s recalled by Colin Charsley, whose father and grandfather produced amateur pantomimes at the theatre. 'I was a Friday night regular at Knightstone in pre-television days. Very often we used to go as a family – in those days it was the social hub of the town. I remember Julie Andrews' voice was absolutely brilliant. Norman Wisdom was in a show called *Out of the Blue* at Easter in 1948. As he sang *Paper Doll* he tore up a newspaper and then leant down and propped up one of the legs of the microphone with it. He had come down from Scarborough with the show and from Weston went into stardom almost overnight.' Wisdom was prophetically described as a 'find' by the *Weston Mercury,* which praised his dynamism and 'vastly amusing facial contortions'. It was in Scarborough that he had bought a deliberately tight-fitting check suit and cloth cap in a second-hand clothes shop for use in his act and his famous accident-prone Gump character was born. Colin also recalled a young comic who

AT KNIGHTSTONE.

We can't believe our own eyes!

WELL, would you believe it! In Weston-super-Mare this week is the tallest man in the world, a midget who has to stretch himself to top a yard-stick, an artist who has no arms, and a gentleman who plays tunes on his xylophone skull.

You don't believe it? Then just pay a visit to Knightstone Theatre and you will see these and many other strange people all on the stage at one and the same time in the Pete Collin's show "Would you beleive it."

The tall gentleman is Lofty, a Dutchman, who is nine feet three and a half inches high and with Pippi, the midget, forms a double act which is well worth your money alone. Then there is El-roy, the artist, who paints, draws, writes, and plays musical instruments with the use of his feet. Another amazing act is provided by Crochet, styled as the mad musician, who allows his head to be thumped with xylophone hammers to produce the latest melodies.

But this is not all. A few sheep take the stage during part of the show and perform various stunts and tricks under the direction of Engler to make an animal act which is as clever as it is polished. Then Fredel keeps the audience in a state of bewilderment as he poses as a wax-dummy in a way which would easily get him a job in any tailor's window, while John Vree and Co. are out to deceive with the aid of a receptacle which can rightly be called a "box of tricks."

A nine-foot Dutchman and performing sheep: the *Weston Gazette* review of an unusual variety show in 1948.

would still be getting laughs with the same routine half-a-century later. 'Ken Dodd would have been in his early twenties. He came on as a one-man-band in pith helmet with a drum on his back and symbols between his knees doing *The Road to Mandalay*. Hutch – the singer Leslie Hutchinson – used to drink for England and sometimes someone had to carry him on and plonk him at the piano as he was pretty legless. I can remember all the old acts – just about anybody who was anybody appeared there. George Hay was very good at his job.'

The variety turns made a lasting impression on thousands of young theatregoers – including 11-year-old Westonian John Cleese. He was one of the last people to see male impersonator Ella Shields, a septuagenarian music hall star, singing her signature number *Burlington Bertie from Bow*, and remembers Douglas 'Cardew' Robinson, who appeared in school uniform with long scarf to the ground and announced he had a longer one but it would look silly. John, who as a comic actor would emulate the success of any of the stars he saw at Knightstone, said: 'My parents took me fairly regularly to see the variety shows. We always sat in the balcony, on stage right. I remember a few of the artistes – Frankie Howerd was the funniest, Bert Shrimpton, Reg Varney and Sid Millward and the Nitwits whom I absolutely loved. Robert Moreton had a surprisingly sophisticated act in which he confused the punch lines of different jokes from his Bumper Fun Book. At Christmas we always went to see the pantomime.'

Norman Wisdom was not the only one to appear when on the cusp of a great career. Morecambe and Wise, still in their mid-20s, were 'a pair of knockabout comedians who keep the fun going at a cracking pace', said a critic. A young Barry Took happened to share a bill with Marty Feldman and Knightstone just might have played a small part in the genesis of their comedy creations *Bootsie and Snudge* and *Round the Horne*. Others were great already. The master of innuendo Max Miller, who starred during the 1949 summer, said: 'All my jokes here tonight have a double meaning – and I can't help what meaning you think of.' He insisted on honouring a booking the following year despite a nasty accident the week before when he suffered a back injury. 'The walk may have been more leisurely and the actions fewer but the wit was as sparkling as ever,' was the verdict.

Weston was incredibly lucky to be effectively on the premier circuit for it meant almost all the top stars in the variety firmament shone down from the stage at one time or another – stars such as Max Wall, Randolph Sutton,

Betty Driver, Cyril Fletcher, Richard Murdoch and Billy Cotton. Entire Bristol Hippodrome bills made Knightstone a convenient next fixture. But it was a different age and artistes were not ambushed at the stage door for autographs as they are today.

Arthur Lucan was Irish washerwoman Old Mother Riley but without wife Kitty McShane, who used to play Riley's daughter in their celebrated double act on film and stage. Lucan was by now nearly 70, had separated from her and was instead supported by Roy Rolland, his understudy who took over the Old Mother Riley role after his death the following year. Michael Miles hosted a stage version of his *Radio Forfeits* with the famous Yes/No Interlude, a favourite part of his later television quiz *Take Your Pick*. It was spontaneous and chaotic, with audience volunteers having to perform as directed if unable to answer his questions. The auditorium reverberated to the exotic sounds of Felix Mendelssohn and his Hawaiian Serenaders, Macari and his Dutch Serenaders, Troise and his Mandoliers and Waldini and his Gypsy Band – though the press doubted whether the South Sea Lovelies backing Mendelssohn were in fact genuine naturally tanned South Sea islanders!

Some acts had to honour commitments across the country between their nightly appearances that would be no mean feat today. Nan Kenway and Douglas Young left bright and early one Thursday morning for a *Workers' Playtime* lunchtime broadcast in Maidstone, Kent, and returned in time for first house at 6.15pm. Bill-topping impressionist Peter Cavanagh surprised audiences by coming on first one evening so he could catch a special flight from Weston airport to London to appear that night at the Albany Club in the presence of the Duke of Edinburgh, who had particularly asked to see him. Cavanagh claimed he was the only impressionist to have permission to impersonate a member of the royal family – namely, the Duke!

The theatre needed a facelift and in early 1951 local firm Field and Wilkins filled the entire auditorium with scaffolding to refresh the décor. The proscenium received a motif of sea shells and fish while crusader tapestries on the wings were replaced with neat fluting and concealed lights. The council, responsible for the building exterior, installed floodlights and strip lighting in the ramparts after obtaining permission for such use of electricity from the Government, necessary because of national power shortages that had continued since the war.

Some of the record August Bank Holiday crowds two years later caught

A George Hay pantomime: *Jack and the Beanstalk* in 1948-9.

the last performances of *Educating Archie,* a stage version of the popular radio show starring ventriloquist Peter Brough and 'Archie Andrews'. Brough had been on radio too long and tried to hide obvious lip movements behind a large BBC microphone, but a forgiving audience was content just to hear Archie's distinctive voice. The next week a 'female' vent, Bobbie Kimber, returned to Weston having started out in Will Godfrey's Troubadour Follies in the canvas sands pavilion near the Grand Pier in 1936. He had begun his career with separate female impersonation and ventriloquism turns but one day did not have time to change back to his male clothes so just grabbed his doll 'Augustus Peabody' and went on stage. Kimber realised he was onto something and found success with his unique hybrid act on television and at the London Palladium.

Arturo Steffani's Silver Songsters boy choir in grey shirts and black shorts formed a pyramid for their spectacular opening number before singing a range of heavenly melodies. With them, ex-Steffani chorister turned solo artiste Ronnie Ronalde, who billed himself simply as Ronalde for greater impact on posters, sang and yodelled, then whistled bird song

KNIGHTSTONE THEATRE
Tel.   WESTON-SUPER-MARE   75

PUSS IN BOOTS

Pantomime Season 1949/50

Our Biggest,
Brightest & Best
Pantomime

PUSS IN BOOTS

Book by DAVID GRAVES
Produced by GEORGE HAY
Associate Producer and Dance
Arranger SYDNEY BARNES

Scenery specially designed and
painted for this Production by
JAMES FREDRICKS
Costumes designed by SYDNEY
BARNES and made in the
Knightstone Theatre Wardrobe
under his direction.
Masks by PETER HALL

A Large Cast of Pantomime Favourites including :-

DAVID GRAVES
as "Penelope"—A peculiar Postma'am"

ARCHIE WALLEN
as "Willie"—Dotty, but docile.

PHYLLIS TERRELL
as "Colin"—our Hero

"DAWN"
as "Gretchen"

MARGARET KENT
as "Trixie"—(Puss in Boots)

KEN WILSON
as "Nimble"

CHARLES ADEY
as "King Regis"

GEORGE SYLVESTER
as "Jonathan Joblot"

SYDNEY BARNES
as "Batswing"—The Wickedest Witch Ever

BRIAN GATES & W. OLLIFFE
as "Titus" the Donkey.

JEANETTE MILLETT
as Principal Dancer

BERTIE ROBBINS
as "Skippy" the little Gnome

THE MAVDOR DANCERS | **THE MAVDOR BABES**

THE TWO PLAYBOYS
STAN KEWLEY & LES MURPHY as "Chips" and "Quips"—Bad lads of a good family

SPECIALITIES BY

CHARLES ADEY & DAWN
KEN WILSON

THE 3 METEORS
THE 2 PLAYBOYS

Orchestra directed by CLIFF BRYAN

with extraordinary virtuosity. 'If there were any birds in the vicinity they must have slipped away to hide their heads in shame,' remarked the *Gazette*.

Britain's greatest harmonica player Ronald Chesney, who became a television comedy scriptwriter, gave away scores of miniature eight-note harmonicas at each performance and taught the audience how to play them. His wife held up a card saying either Blow or Suck as Chesney played his own harmonica. The instruments were supplied free by maker Hohner and had Chesney's name inscribed on them.

The top stars were called on to judge rounds of the Modern Venus beauty contest, started in 1945 by Edward Turner at the request of the War Office that was looking for British pin-ups to replace outworn Hollywood portraits for forces' magazines. Dozens of bathing-suited beauties competed in front of vast holiday crowds at The Pool over six weeks for a prize worth £5. Famously now, Swindon 13-year-old Diana Fluck, who became film star Diana Dors, reached third place in an early round. The first year was so popular, with 18,000 spectators in total, that it was made an annual event and became an almost mandatory appointment for visiting artistes, who included Laurel and Hardy during their Hippodrome week in 1947. Not that any needed coercion.

But a long shadow was being cast over these blissful times. As Frankie Howerd pulled in holiday crowds and topped the bill at an Odeon midnight matinee in aid of Lynmouth flood victims in 1952, a 750ft transmitter on a hilltop 14 miles away in Wenvoe, South Wales, began beaming BBC television programmes to the West Country for the first time. Long queues always greeted the opening of Chamberlain Hall in Locking Road where throughout the day at least 100 people could be found glued to 15 working sets, and every night lights blazed in shops selling the newfangled things on attractive hire purchase terms. Those on the rocky outcrop must have felt a distinct chill down their spines at this upstart rival for their paying public. Theatre variety was facing a death sentence, and while the Queen's coronation in June 1953 sent TV sales into orbit, that only hastened the inevitable. Weston commemorated the coronation with a £6,000 landscaped area and perimeter path at Knightstone. Henceforth, Coronation Gardens became a place on the town map.

The first suggestion that an awkwardly narrow and long market hall in High Street could become the town centre theatre everyone desired emerged in

1945, to great scepticism that it could even begin to replace Knightstone. The council fitted a false ceiling, covered the walls with heavy hessian drapes and laid wooden tiers on the flat stone floor. Sure enough, when The Playhouse opened in June 1946 it sat only 500, and while it was described as just a concert hall Knightstone directors feared it could poach enough of their business to do real harm without being viable itself. Even more rudimentary competition arrived in 1949 with the seasonal Arena Theatre, a 500-seat tent pitched on a Beach Road bomb-site, which had a penchant for Shakespeare and blowing down in the wind. A noble experiment, it lasted just five years before the land was put up for sale.

Buoyed by the success of their house pantomime, the creative Knightstone team turned their hand to high season resident shows, starting in 1946 with *Summer Rhapsody*, produced and musically directed by Hay, with Sydney Barnes in charge of dancing. A different guest each week, including Robb Wilton, Hutch, Ronald Frankau, Herschel Henlere, Adelaide Hall and Suzette Tarri, starred alongside a talented permanent cast headed by Frank O'Brian. The orchestra was boosted with a second grand piano and brilliant light from two new carbon arc spotlights picked out every facial expression. In an example of its engaging originality, when anyone returned late to their seat after an interval the show was stopped and the company advanced to the footlights to explain the entire plot to the embarrassed patron. Audiences loved it and extra seats were crammed into the aisles for a glittering performance to end the 13-week run. Guest stars judged different rounds of the Modern Venus competition and when Robb Wilton announced the overall winner with his unique dry humour he had a poolside crowd of 7,000 in hysterics.

Summer Rhapsody had gone head-to-head with the first Playhouse summer production, *Frivolities*, one critic marvelling that not many resorts had two top-notch resident shows. But while rivalry between the theatres was harmonious with holiday crowds in town, relations soured when they vied for smaller winter audiences. Gordon Lane lodged an official complaint after the council announced repertory for the Playhouse at a time when Knightstone had booked Harry Hanson's Court Players. Weston wasn't big enough for both. The press accused the council of being unfair and unsporting to its own tenants, a view echoed by the mayor Alderman Craig who warned there was no point in waging a form of guerrilla warfare. In the end the decision backfired on the council, for it lost money while Knightstone

Bertie Robbins as King of Hearts and Sydney Barnes relishing his title role in 1951 pantomime *Queen of Hearts*, for which he also designed the costumes.

Sydney Barnes and George Hay.

takings were reasonable.

Summer Rhapsody's return the following year with Nan Kenway and Douglas Young was another class act from The Three Musketeers. Actually it was increasingly just Hay and his d'Artagnan Sydney Barnes: George Bosley was fully engaged as the new mayor and sadness befell the town that December with the death of Gordon Lane. Long before running Knightstone he had been a light singer and entertainment pioneer and his obituary said no man had ever done so much for Weston theatre. He rarely agreed with his co-directors but their frankness, which he welcomed, was perpetual mental stimulus. Lane mentored his stepson Raymond at Knight-stone from lowly programme-seller to assistant manager but did not live to see his meteoric rise to manage the London Coliseum and a host of other Stoll Moss theatres.

After a few years bachelor Hay, a tall, shy man who seldom gave press interviews, moved the flamboyant and amusing Barnes in with him in his two-floor flat in the right-hand tower. It was a close relationship generally accepted by those around them. Sharing the flat was Hay's mischievous budgerigar Billie who was allowed to fly around. In the costume department he would perch on a sewing machine, eyeing another thimble to snatch, fly off with and hide. When his antics got too disruptive he was returned to his cage, which disgusted him. Pantomime star Wyn Calvin recalled: 'The budgerigar used to talk. Sometimes he was kept in a cage in the box office and when the phone rang he would say: "It's a rotten show, it's a rotten show." As George Hay was having breakfast one morning the phone went. He left the table to answer it and when he came back the budgerigar was basting in his fried egg.' Barnes could often be found sketching intricate designs faithfully turned into pantomime costumes by chief seamstress Lillian Smedley and assistants Edith Wilson and Jessie Smith. Before showtime Hay was always front of house, greeting patrons with a genial 'good evening'. In a Sunday afternoon tradition the elegantly tailored pair strolled the promenade together, offering acquaintances a stately tilt of the head and polite 'hello', eager for reaction to the latest production. But behind the Edwardian manners lurked caustic wit – Barnes remarking that one elderly actress was 'held together with spit'.

Harry Secombe, Reg 'Confidentially' Dixon, Ronnie Ronalde, Jimmy Young and Cyril Fletcher starred in the 1954 holiday line-up and 15-year-old Terry Counsell had the enviable task of meeting them all in his after-school-hours job operating one of the carbon arc spotlights, known as limes. He recalled: 'Harry Secombe was a fantastic character. He sat in the audience one night watching the show when they were looking for him to go on. When he realised, instead of going on from backstage he went on from the front. He was very popular and did his shaving routine.' Terry had to note down the 'lighting plot' – the stars' lighting requirements. 'You asked them what colour they wanted and any cues for a song change or music change. They were all old pros and most of them were very under-standing.' While operating the lime the distance between two carbon rods which produced the intense arc light had to be regularly adjusted as they burnt down, but the light could eventually go out, plunging the subject into sudden gloom, as happened frequently. Terry then had to open the lamp and use pliers to replace the red-hot rods while an operator on the other spot covered for him. 'I used to get six shillings a night for two shows, and if there were six nights it was a lot of money. I got more working evenings than I did for my day job after leaving school of apprentice electrician. It was a paying hobby which I loved doing – it was another world.'

Backstage wasn't entirely a male domain. Several women operated the spotlights over the years, Terry having taken over from Wyn Goodyear, who by day ran a public library above Boots the chemist. Twenty-year-old Yvonne Williams, a dancer since she was four, dreamt of a stage career but settled for working the spotlight rather than appearing in it while her husband Lauri was chief stage electrician. Recruitment could be through family or just by bumping into someone, as happened to Reg and Beryl Byles at a Boxing Day dance in the Winter Gardens. Reg had appeared in British Legion pantomimes and knew Knightstone stage manager Rex Hughes, who wanted a volunteer. Beryl said: 'I heard Reg say "Beryl will do it"!' So began a playful stint in the lime box. 'In *Babes in the Wood* we usually had just a few leaves falling on the babes asleep under a tree in the forest to represent the passing of time, but on the last night I bribed one of the stagehands to pour two sackfuls of leaves, given to us by the parks department. On another occasion I got a stagehand to use a real egg instead of a trick one when it had to be hit over someone's head. The actor was most upset.'

The limes were housed in an external cabin on the flat roof between the front towers, where the pre-war film projectors had been located. This had to be accessed through the costume department in the left tower, which now doubled as a rehearsal room. The stage manager could speak instructions to the operators by baby alarm but they could not reply, typical of Knightstone improvisation. Communication with the lighting board operator, perched on a platform 6ft above the stage manager's corner, was even more rudimentary and could involve a rolled-up newspaper or long stick to signal a cue, since there was no cue light. As a contingency when national power cuts loomed in 1967, electricians rigged up four car headlamps powered by two car batteries in a wheelbarrow, which was placed downstage. Someone sat in the front row ready to operate the Heath Robinson device – which

In 1911 the Dimo-Panto company staged *Cinderella*, produced by Rosina Dimoline, standing far left. Two of her daughters played the leads, Marjorie (Cinderella) and Eunice (The Prince), centre left and right. Wilfred Roe (Ugly Sister) is fifth from right, middle row. The cast was pictured in front of the pavilion.

was used for 20 minutes on one occasion. Electrician Pete Magor recalled an extraordinary coincidence in another show. 'One time we pulled the lever to black out the stage and when we put it back nothing happened. Unbeknown to us there was a power cut at that point and half of Weston had gone out, but we were panicking because we thought the board had gone wrong. It was a bit strange.' Four decades earlier when the lighting failed during a play, shops were besieged for candles and within 35 minutes the performance resumed with the makeshift illumination. The title of the play was *By Candlelight*.

News of the sensational 1944 house pantomime spread rapidly and demand to see the second was overwhelming. Some rural bookings were for groups of 400 and one party had to charter a train from Chard. Special pantomime buses were laid on from Bristol, a gratifying turning of tables on a big-city rival. *Dick Whittington and his Cat* was opulent entertainment with magnificent settings, slick production and top-class speciality acts and would have been a triumph even in the West End, said the *Gazette*.

Year by year their popularity grew. Despite post-war scarcity the wardrobe department delivered dazzling shows, stitching together bits and pieces and transforming old costumes into something new. More than 35,000 saw the 51 performances of *Mother Goose* in 1947 and on stage at

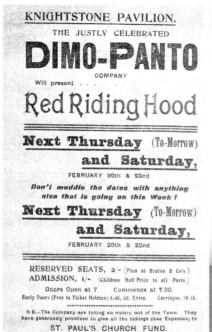

Victor Dimoline, star of Dimo-Panto and British Legion pantomimes, with 'Algie'.

the end Mr Bosley declared it the most successful pantomime in the theatre's history. The next year the wardrobe ladies began preparing in early autumn for *Jack and the Beanstalk*, taking a week to make a knight's shimmering costume out of silver discs for Jack. The chorus wore specially painted costumes that glowed under ultra-violet light. Pantomime excursion trains ran and the last normal service for Taunton left Weston 25 minutes later than usual. Knightstone, as so often before, had the power to change the railway timetable! Now the audience was 40,000 and in 1949 records were smashed again when 54,000 saw *Puss in Boots*. With the Playhouse closed at the time, Knightstone was the only theatre open between Bristol and Exeter and on the last night 72 coaches surged in from just about every-where, clogging the streets and Bosley's Melrose Café car park where he ensured a snack bar opened late as part of the service. Magistrates had granted permission for up to 40 coach drivers to stand in the theatre balcony to await their homebound passengers.

Standards were never allowed to slip: Hay, who composed some of the music, insisted on genuine stories and David Graves obliged with original scripts, meticulously researched and crafted. The shows were never better than on first night, a Christmas Eve or Boxing Day, when the fun could last until 11pm before the discipline of two performances daily and three on Saturdays forced reluctant cuts in running time. On those marathon Saturdays, with starting times of 2pm, 5pm and 8pm, audiences could total 3,000. Practically the entire population of some places saw them and wider Weston reaped the benefit. Many arrived in early afternoon and looked round the shops before attending second house; others saw the matinee and spent the evening in town. Letters of appreciation flooded in and plenty wanted to book the same seat on the same night the following year.

To avoid repetition the little-known *Queen of Hearts* was chosen for 1951. David Graves researched fairy-tale lore at the British Museum on which to base an authentic script. Hay always sought innovation and was impressed with the novelty of 3D cinema fascinating audiences at the Festival of Britain. Ingeniously he was able to introduce the effect live on stage. A pair of 3D glasses was handed out with every programme, promising a thrilling new experience for Knightstone-goers. In a scene where a knave stole tarts and threw them at the audience, everyone ducked because it seemed they were headed straight for their faces. Dangling caterpillars, butterflies and insects looked as if they were dancing before their eyes.

Old King Cole in 1952 was the most lavish and expensive production yet and so many bookings poured in the run was extended to a record eight weeks before it began. Sydney Barnes revelled in his myriad roles – associate producer, dance arranger, costume designer and Mother Hubbard. Singer Randolph Sutton [Ran], in the title role, had been so impressed with the pantomimes' outstanding reputation that he had asked to take part, and it attracted his immense native Bristol fanbase. Once again David Graves wrote a witty script and James Fredricks' opening backcloth was a dramatic view resembling Dunster Castle as traditional local reference. Stage manager George Wyatt created a wealth of props and when George Hay casually remarked 'Oh, and I shall want 16 violins' he saw it as a challenge to produce them. Lighting was upgraded for special effects and seamstresses spent months stitching 100,000 sequins onto costumes. Wyn Calvin, who played the Wizard, said: 'Everyone on a Saturday in those days would have come in from the country. Ran said someone sitting down there had a firkin of cider. I didn't know whether he was being rude or not. One day the principal boy was rushed to hospital in the interval with a grumbling appendix – a phrase I had never heard before. Ran said *he* had a travelling fart! He was playing Old King Cole whose daughter was being married to the principal boy. He said he would stand in for the principal boy and as he walked down stage with his daughter to the wedding music he turned to us and said "Incest, incest!"'

Appetite for pantomime seemed insatiable, for amateur productions in aid of the British Legion that followed in January or February never suffered – and were even extended from three days in the early years to ten days with matinees to cope with their own runaway success. In a huge patriotic surge of enthusiasm after the war British Legion branches from across Somerset snapped up tickets as soon as they went on sale in October. Once the police had to be called to clear Knightstone Causeway, choked with fans queueing for any returned tickets.

Those celebrated shows had humble origins decades earlier in a fairy play staged one Christmas by the Dimoline family in the loft of their home. They were pillars of St Paul's Church whose curate persuaded them to perform at the church hall to fund-raise for a new church building. Their popularity grew and in 1908, now as the Dimo-Panto Company, they presented *Red Riding Hood* to full houses at Knightstone and on the Grand Pier and enjoyed continued success in the run-up to the First World War. The shows were produced by matriarch Rosina Dimoline, who fully involved her children Eunice, Iris, Marjorie and Victor. One evening in 1933 as Victor, a life member of Weston Dramatic Society, reminisced with fellow actor Wilfred Roe about those early days, they decided to do one more pantomime for old time's sake. *Babes in the Wood* with amateur cast, some of whom had never been on stage before, was so successful it led to another and another – in fact, 19 in all. Victor had entertained troops in the Great War with a ventriloquist act, the Army having paid for his doll 'Algie', and he donated pantomime profits to the British Legion and St Dunstan's Homes for Blinded Soldiers.

Auditions were open to all, but the prospect daunted 16-year-old Doris Foreman who twice pulled out before plucking up courage to go. It was the start of more than 50 years on the amateur stage, from pantomime chorus

Leslie Powell, Don Charlsey and Leslie Titley in a scene from 1950 British Legion pantomime *Red Riding Hood*. Weston council was often the butt of jokes: the signpost points to the council chamber in one direction and Utopia in the opposite direction! The Austin Seven was on loan from Don's son Colin.

to opera star. 'I went and never looked back. One learnt so much from watching those more experienced. You learnt how to throw away lines, asides, and to cope with ad-libs, which comedians are notorious for. Diction was polished, particularly attention to ends of words. I remember one dress rehearsal – it was past midnight and I had not arrived home. My anxious father rang Knightstone Theatre and spoke to George Hay who returned to the phone with a message from the producer Wilfred Roe: "When the entrances and exits are perfected they will be allowed home."'

Unlike professionals, the principals had no microphones, so voices had to carry to the back stalls over a full orchestra, conducted in different years by George Hay, Lemuel Kinsey, George Locke, Leon Godby and Eric Austin, with Jessica Hillman on piano. Dancers aged six to 16 were trained

KNIGHTSTONE THEATRE
WESTON-SUPER-MARE
Lessees : KNIGHTSTONE THEATRE, Ltd.   Phone : 75   Man. Dir. GEORGE HAY
'Week commencing MONDAY, MAY 24th
MONDAY to FRIDAY at 8.0   SATURDAY at 5.45 & 8.30
PRICES : 4/6, 3/6, 2/6 Res.   1/6 Unres.   BOX OFFICE OPEN DAILY from 10 a.m.

A stage version of radio's *The Archers* was presented in 1954 by a cast that included Gretchen Franklin.

for the productions by sisters Joline and Judythe Alexander at their Alexander School of Dancing in Hill Road. Joline also choreographed for the Operatic Society until her death at the age of 77.

Scripts mixed pantomime fantasy with local satire, such as the Weston railway station scene in which the mayor of Weston, played by Keith Tyler, was disappointed to find that the visiting mayor of Loch Ness (Frank Eager) had not brought the Loch Ness monster with him for placing in Marine Lake. Asked if he had ever seen the Loch Ness monster, the mayor of Loch Ness replied: 'Yes, I married her!'

In local amateur tradition speeches and gifts sealed each run and there was a great roar at the end of *Robinson Crusoe* when the Cannibal King (Leslie Titley) was handed a neatly tied present of seaweed. After the shows special buses acted as free taxis, taking everyone practically to their doors.

Doris Foreman and Leslie A Scamp in the joint Weston Operatic Society and
Red Triangle Players production of *Call Me Madam* in 1956.

Hay nurtured all the amateur groups, allotting them their own season, sharing round attractive dates to avoid favouritism and reducing hire charges if he had had a prosperous summer. He was as accommodating to repertory companies – if out of pragmatism. Keith Salberg, who two years earlier at 17 had become Britain's youngest theatrical manager, recalled his eight-strong company sheltering from savage weather in Forte's Café on Knightstone Road before rehearsals one morning, where they ironically pondered slow ticket sales. 'The winds were howling outside and we said to each other: "I wonder why it is we don't get more people coming in at night?" You didn't get big audiences there in the winter. Theatres took these rep companies because it was the cheapest way of running a theatre at the seaside in the winter. Before we opened the amateurs were there with *Jane Eyre* and they got the audience in one week that we got spread over four. We worked on a percentage on sharing terms with the management but it didn't really pay.'

On their first visit the company stayed at the Grosvenor Hotel but the

Joline Alexander   Jessica Hillman

next time, in reduced circumstances, they used one of town's guest houses, which had their share of formidable landladies. Phillip Barrett's company arrived with ten truckloads of scenery and a 17-year-old guest star, John Clark, smitten with 21-year-old leading lady Elizabeth Digby-Smith. John, who had been radio's first *Just William*, recalled: 'Elizabeth and I were quite close, although she was older and more experienced than me. We shared digs but had a rather nosy and interfering landlady. Elizabeth was about to give me a sex class when an imperious voice came all the way down the corridor from the landlady's room for me to immediately leave the leading lady's room, or else. It never happened again. Probably the cider.'

John married Lynn Redgrave of the famous acting dynasty whose youngest member, John Redgrave, was a 12-year-old props hand at the theatre when his mother Angela starred as principal girl in *Dick Whittington and his Cat*. He recalls: 'I was supposed to earn £7 10s a week, which I thought was an amazing amount of money. Then George Hay discovered how old I was and said he would pay me £1. I used to be sent to the kitchens of the Melrose Café every morning with a biscuit tin to collect that day's dough for the slosh scenes. And it was heavy too! In the slosh scenes the dame and the comedians got covered in gunge. But the funniest thing was trying to get scenery into the theatre when it was windy. Three or four times it blew into the Marine Lake and we had to fish it out and dry it.'

The 1955 Christmas pantomime was inexplicably the first in 11 years not produced by George Hay or dressed by his wardrobe department. *Babes in the Wood*, with no high-profile names, was fully imported. 'Pantomime is dying, stabbed through the heart by the television tubes,' mourned the *Mercury*. Two months later Hay lost his co-director, benefactor and indefatigable supporter. George Bosley had been a highly regarded entertainer, businessman and mayor and at his funeral service the borough mace was draped in black crepe. It was clear an era was ending and although the theatre still managed another variety summer, the highlight was fittingly *Thanks for the Memory* that reunited legends of music hall – singers GH Elliott, Hetty King and Randolph Sutton, comic Billy Danvers and ventriloquist Johnson Clark.

Nevertheless the announcement in February 1957 that, after 18 years, the management was not renewing its lease still came as a bombshell. As Hay and Barnes retired together to Bournemouth, Weston was left to reflect on their remarkable achievement. With Bosley and Lane they had been the first to make Knightstone an economic proposition. They had presented entertainment of West End calibre, created the town's own superb repertory company and provided unflagging encouragement to amateur performers. In the process they had sustained and invigorated the local tourist industry and it would feel their loss.

New Look

One reason for the tenants' departure might have been the long list of overdue repairs. A council team sent in to inspect the building was so horrified at its condition they wanted to close it down immediately. The original gas pipes had corroded, wiring was dangerous and gangway carpets were riddled with holes. It would cost a small fortune to put right, at a time when the Government was urging utmost caution in public spending. Knightstone could easily have gone the way of hundreds of doomed variety houses but as it was indispensable to the holiday economy the council decided to operate it for the next ten years and approved an urgent £12,000 modernisation programme. A dilapidations claim was sent to the old management.

During an initial three-month closure, amateur groups were dismayed to find themselves consigned to the Playhouse. Doris Foreman (now Doris Wilsher) said: 'At the old Playhouse there was a tunnel you had to go through from backstage to front. It was a very old building with no good wings or facilities. The Knightstone wasn't posh – the principal dressing-room had an old settee, nothing was particularly updated – but it had everything you wanted. I much preferred the Knightstone – it had atmosphere.'

Knightstone's doors re-opened on Easter Saturday 1957 to reveal multi-coloured strip lighting and shell-shaped wall lamps in the foyer and new carpets, stage floor and curtains. The bar was more roomy and comfortable and the buffet had been redecorated. Topping the bill was 25-year-old singer Des O'Connor, who had the promise of a successful career, said the *Mercury*. 'He has an attractive personality, his patter is good material and he was extremely popular with Monday's first night audience.' That variety week was immediately followed by another shut-down when hundreds of comfortable tip-up seats were installed, the central gangway was eliminated and balcony seats re-positioned to face the stage so audiences didn't constantly have to crook their necks.

The final improvements a year later were the most striking. Theatregoers had long complained of poor views and often sat in the cheaper, raised back stalls. Now all the stalls were raked, but at the price of auditorium capacity reduced to 950. A new box office and covered queueing area changed the look of the entrance while at the rear a new stage door and scene dock area effectively increased the stage size. On the side of the theatre overlooking Marine Lake a refurbished Harbour Café served patrons and passers-by. Not everyone welcomed the changes. Terry Counsell thought the décor destroyed the traditional atmosphere. 'When the town took it over unfortunately they redecorated it in pale colours and it lost its ambience. It didn't smell like a theatre any more – you used to be able to smell the greasepaint. It became too clean.'

The 1957 summer saw the start of the era of resident shows, in town for the season. Knightstone had all but given up on weekly variety: top names charged too much and without them the box office suffered. In seasonal shows different programmes were rotated frequently so holidaymakers could visit several times without seeing the same thing.

They began with *Gaytime,* presented by Yorkshire impresario Hedley Claxton at resorts around the country. In Weston it was usually fronted by affable brothers Bob and Alf Pearson, a veteran music hall act who sang popular ballads with Bob at the piano. This first of five over consecutive summers had been booked for the Playhouse but was switched to Knightstone with augmented cast. The brothers led a vivacious company of 16 comics, singers, musicians and dancers in a lavish once-nightly show with five programmes that changed on Tuesdays and Fridays during a record run for Knightstone of three months. The *Mercury* heaped praise on the production: the Pearsons were 'vital, musical, amusing, full of personality – so immensely and engagingly alive'. Billy Baxter was a young comedian said to be destined for a brilliant career, enormously funny and different every time he appeared. Valerie Gray and Arthur Downes were fine-quality singers and Gwenda Wilkin was hailed as one of the world's leading accordionists. It was deemed the best seaside show in Britain – there was even admiration for the high standard of props. Some of its popularity might have been down to Old Lady Gaytime, the nickname for a 1933 Morris 10 car that stage manager Robert Ash had bought for £20 that summer. Vividly decorated it toured Brean and Burnham-on-Sea publicising the show but kept breaking down and eventually blew up at a crossroads, collapsing with a clatter of parts in true theatrical fashion. Mr Claxton promised a replacement and contributed spiritual support as well, pinning up a philosophical and humorous Prayer for the Success of the Resident Show that ended 'May the spirit of this company be the spirit of good troupers, and if we can last until the end of September I will not look any further.' His prayer was answered for

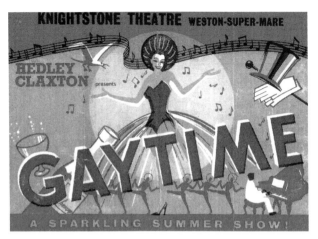

Hedley Claxton's *Gaytime* summer show ran from 1957 to 1961. Singing brothers Bob and Alf Pearson were the headline stars from 1957 to 1960.

they did indeed stay until then.

But well-supported shows were now the exception. The expensive modernisation had been a brave face on a deep crisis: television had almost wiped out off-season patronage. In 1958 ITV arrived in the West Country and, for the first time since the war, Knightstone was, in total, closed for more than half the year. After *Jack and the Beanstalk* played to two weeks of sparse houses a dispirited Claxton took to the stage to warn a wider audience: 'In Weston now you have a municipal theatre comparable to any in any seaside resort throughout the British Isles and it is only by adequate support that these things can be kept going for you.'

The reproof had little effect. Two weeks later saw the last British Legion pantomime, the nine performances of *Babes in the Wood* being so poorly attended the players could barely afford the traditional end-of-run party. A last chance for variety, in an experimental early season slot, failed, as did a series of Bournemouth Symphony Orchestra concerts, despite guest appearances by distinguished conductors Charles Groves, George Hurst, James Robertson, Myer Fredman, Constantin Silvestri and Alceo Galliera. An attempt at pantomime by Geoffrey Hewitson's Famous Players was a disaster even with a creditable performance in the lead role by Peter Adamson, the future Len Fairclough in *Coronation Street*.

Not only had local support evaporated but the town was becoming less a staying resort, and many who did stay brought tents or caravans and their own food; all they spent was two shillings on a parking fee. Hotels and guest houses were advised to cut their tariffs to fill vacancies.

The fact was there was a new kid on the block and it gave still gas-lit Weston a rude awakening. In 1958 Tommy Steele's 16-year-old brother Colin Hicks and his Cabin Boys headed a pulsating bill of stars from *Six-Five Special*, the BBC's first rock-and-roll programme, on the Odeon stage one Sunday night and hundreds of excited youths jostled for tickets. Weston already had a vibrant music scene but teenage culture was revolutionary and everyone wondered whatever was next, some believing it would lead to juvenile delinquency. The immediate answer was that the very next month the real thing – the *Six-Five Special* television programme itself – was broadcast live from the Winter Gardens Pavilion, if with a less-frenetic Johnny Duncan and his Blue Grass Boys and the Ray Ellington Quartet. It was a pointer to a very different future on which the council was slow to capitalise and the Odeon was left to make the running.

Tom O'Connor in
Gaytime in 1959.

At least Knightstone could rely on *Gaytime*, which broke records in 1959, the house-full boards a regular sight over its 14 weeks, and show posters covered the town. As in the previous year the Pearsons were joined by 'The Effervescent Comedian' Ken Roberts. Oddly for a show noted for set-piece spectaculars, only three musicians occupied the pit. Marjorie West and Raymond Paul played the theatre's two baby grand pianos, placed so they could see each other, while Tom O'Connor used his own drums. Tom, a 23-year-old Australian on his first British theatrical engagement, thought Knightstone offered just the right atmosphere. '*Gaytime* was a company show and it was like belonging to a close family, with no one having a "star complex". This also brought the audience closer to the performers. Some of Weston's residents must have seen the five different shows many times over and there were few, if any, empty seats. We would sometimes be invited to social events by regular members of the audience.' Indeed, one local resident was reported to have seen the show 30 times and taken friends each time.

A gift was presented to the oldest father and a bouquet to the oldest mother in every audience and by the end of the run a 97-year-old man had been the very oldest recipient. For Claxton it was one of the happiest of seasons, but there had been a desperately sad time when one of the company, Terry Kendall, heard that his glamorous film star daughter Kay Kendall,

> ## KNIGHTSTONE THEATRE
> Nightly at 8 p.m.
> ## GAYTIME
> With All-Star Cast including
> ### BOB & ALF PEARSON
> ### and KEN ROBERTS
> **COMPLETE CHANGE OF PROGRAMME EVERY TUESDAY AND FRIDAY**
>
> Programme No. 1 includes :
>   ' Rocking Round the Clock,' ' The Jolson Story,' ' Violin Ballet.'
>
> Programme No. 2 includes :
>   ' Oldtime Music Hall,' ' Calypso,' ' Roses.'
>
> Programme No. 3 includes :
>   ' Circus Days,' ' Let's go Shopping,' ' Study in Black and White.'
>
> Programme No. 4 includes :
>   '' Jungle Fantasy,' ' Sunny Side Up,' ' Toy-maker's Dream.'
>
> Programme No. 5 includes :
>   ' In Old Vienna,' ' Flying High,' ' Autumn Concerto.'
>
> All Seats Bookable: 3/6, 4/6, 5/6, 6/6, 7/6
> Box Office: Tel. 75

The different *Gaytime* programmes in 1960.

wife of actor Rex Harrison, had died at the age of 32 from leukaemia. He had not even known she was ill. Terry's sick wife Doric, with whom he had been a song-and-dance act, also died shortly after. 'Things must go on, that's show business,' he said, with commendable outward calm.

During the season Ronnie Hancox, whose dance band were Winter Gardens regulars, had fronted a weekly *Sunday Showtime* with a 20-year-old singer he had hired on a three-year training contract with no experience required. With her talent and good looks Susan Maughan soon found fame on radio and television and charted with the catchy *Bobby's Girl* in 1962.

From a summer high Knightstone sunk to a new low, with no show over Christmas or the New Year for the first time since the war. The council bowed to hoteliers' demands for a longer holiday season by extending the 1960 *Gaytime* from 14 to 17 weeks and adding a further week during the run. Claxton pondered replacing the entire cast for fresh impetus, contacting leading agents and scouring the country for suitable artistes, but most were too expensive or unavailable. In the end he kept the same people but changed the format with different curtains, new music and original scenes. Loyal fans in fact wanted the Pearsons and Ken Roberts back and had told him so in no uncertain terms. Repeat visits saw takings rise and Claxton concluded that, far from growing tired of the same faces, audiences greeted them as friends.

Modern Venus

Bob and Alf Pearson judged Joy Barlow the winner of the Modern Venus
beauty contest at The Pool in 1958.

The old team didn't disappoint. The Pearsons were as vibrant as ever, making no fewer than 19 costume changes. Consummate comedian Ken Roberts paraded a variety of amusing characters, New Zealand baritone Ronald Maconaghie and Jean Anderson's duets were charming and Gwenda Wilkin received one of the biggest ovations, even if her dog in the dressing-room howled the place down whenever she played Liszt's Hungarian Rhapsody! A summer season had 'never got away to such a dashing, exhilarating start. It is the modern seaside show at its finest, staged with a lavishness that fully meets the present-day taste for spectacle,' remarked the *Mercury*. Long box office queues guaranteed another bumper season and by mid-August income was up nearly 40 per cent on the year before, although the 1960 season did begin three weeks earlier. One Cardiff pensioner wrote that it was a two-hour tonic even a doctor could not prescribe.

But in direct contradiction to his earlier findings that suggested he should stick with the same cast, Claxton replaced the Pearsons with The Four Jones Boys – un-related singers from Bath – to appeal to a younger crowd for his final *Gaytime* in 1961, which at just over 18 weeks remained the longest run ever for a Knightstone show. Claxton said it had to keep up with the times while retaining the *Gaytime* formula but he had sought to strike a balance so as not to lose older fans. He paid the price at the box office. New leading lady, singer Christine Yates, recalled: 'Ken Roberts was a very funny comic, so good in sketches, but the company had less discipline and sometimes the dancers were all over the place.' One day pianist Raymond Paul was taken ill, which was bad enough, but disastrously colleague Marjorie West also fell ill two days later, leaving just the drummer in the pit. A pianist rushed in from the Ronnie Hancox Band spent all day frantically rehearsing the many numbers to save the show that night. It was an example of the friendly co-operation that existed between musicians at council venues, who interchanged as necessary between the Rozel Bandstand, Winter Gardens and Knightstone.

Now Claxton's five-year contract was up the council looked to other promoters for famous television personalities he was never able to deliver. *Gaytime* had been popular but its stars were seen as old-fashioned and the family show concept dated. The biggest names that summer had actually appeared on Sundays. An experimental series of concerts called *Make Mine Music*, after the radio programme that starred singer David Hughes, had to be cancelled before they began because he suffered a heart attack and could not appear. Ronnie Hancox came to the rescue again, bringing back *Sunday Showtime* with a different guest each week, including Joe 'Mr Piano' Henderson, Ken Dodd, Jimmy Young and Bryan Johnson. Jimmy Young, a ballad singer before becoming a popular disc jockey, was the first Knightstone artiste to use a radio microphone, which created a few technical problems but was seen as a step forward. For the next summer show a central, rising microphone was installed but the shear pin had an unfortunate habit of failing, sending it at high speed into the ground, to great audience amusement. Stagehands battled to fix it but had to wait for loud music to drown the banging.

All 400 free tickets were snapped up for a broadcast of general knowledge quiz *Ask Me Another* with chairman Franklin Engelmann and panellist 'farmer' Ted Moult. And Wyn Calvin returned to give budding local performers a chance in the footlights in a one-night stage version of *New Airs and Faces*, the talent-seeking show he presented on TWW. Its 7.45pm start was timed so those from South Wales could catch the 10.15pm steamer back to Cardiff.

As well as the last *Gaytime*, 1961 saw the final British Legion Festival of Remembrance concert, with the British Legion Silver Band, RAF Locking trumpeters and Operatic Society singers Lilian Bailey and Edward Deal accompanied on piano by Jessica Hillman. The concerts had begun in 1948, an unintentionally amusing feature being the presence of just one Chelsea Pensioner, the word being they couldn't afford to fund the travel costs of any more.

A 17-year association now began with Bunny Baron, an ex-wartime troop entertainer who had topped the bill in a variety show at the Playhouse in 1948 and was now a producer of seaside summer shows. Initially he organised pantomimes while fellow impresario Richard Stone, also a former wartime entertainments officer, presented holiday show *Let's Make a Night of It* for four years. These were distinctly different from *Gaytime,* with bigger names in a twice-nightly variety format.

Baron's first production – *Aladdin* with Rosemary Squires at Christmas 1961 – was a gamble by the council having suffered a loss on the previous pantomime and under pressure to make savings. The twice-daily, three-week show was hit by atrocious weather and one day only 93 people saw the two performances. Audiences picked up as conditions improved and its eventual £480 loss was considered a good result in the circumstances. Many attended

Holidaymakers at Marine Lake during a *Gaytime* season.

pantomime last nights especially for the traditional extras. Stagehands made appearances and artistes played jokes on each other, provided it was all in good fun and not taken too far.

For the first *Let's Make a Night of It* the council put up new show poster boards around the theatre and launched a £200 publicity drive in neighbouring towns, confident it bettered anything on offer in Bristol or Bath. Headline comedienne Beryl Reid revelled in the characters she had created on radio – Marlene from Birmingham, pig-tailed schoolgirl Monica from St Trinian's and industrial glamour girl Miss Nuts and Bolts. West Country comedian Billy Burden was as amusing off stage as on, agonising in broad Dorset accent over which script he was supposed to be following, and pop

Hugh Lloyd and Terry Scott 'arriving' for *Let's Make a Night of It* in 1963.

star Craig Douglas, who had topped the charts with *Only Sixteen*, was praised for 'superb artistry'.

There was embarrassment one night when stagehand Lauri Williams pulled the wrong lever and instead of raising the motorised safety curtain after an interval accidentally activated a sprinkler, sending four gallons of water down the curtain, drenching the stage, footlights and pit. Beryl Reid explained the incident to the puzzled audience, adding that the face of the person responsible was glowing bright red. It was not the first time the mistake had been made. Lauri recalled: 'There was no flying room so the asbestos safety curtain had to be rolled up and down on a winch like an old-fashioned clothes wringer. It was operated by levers in a panel at the side of the stage, which also housed similar drencher on and off levers. Obviously the drencher was turned off straight away but the damage had been done. When the curtain was raised it would continue dripping as it was wrapping around the roller for quite a while during the second half, which caused a few problems for the artiste.' It was nearly 'curtains' for Craig Douglas on another night. During the show a stagehand picked up a weight, not realising it was holding a large flat in front of the curtains where Craig was performing. The heavy scenery fell, narrowly missing the singer, who, like a trouper, carried on with his act as if nothing had happened.

Lauri remembers several run-ins with Beryl Reid, irritated at being 'upstaged' by her co-star. 'Billy Burden was getting all the laughs. She insisted she wasn't getting the brightest spotlight and I can remember after one show us arguing like mad about it. She didn't turn up for three nights and someone stood in for her. Then she came in with a couple of bottles of sherry and apologised.'

Throughout August Russ Conway and Dorothy Squires starred in live variety at the Odeon, and with Johnny Dankworth and Gladys Morgan at the Winter Gardens, Vernon Adcock's band at Rozel Bandstand (now being grandly called Rozel Arena Theatre) and Peter Haddon's repertory company at the Playhouse the press remarked that never before had Weston seen such a full bill of topline entertainment. One night Reid and Douglas joined Conway and Squires on radio show *Seaside Night* recorded at the Odeon. Vernon Adcock was a real gentleman who made a cameo appearance in 1964 film *The Beauty Jungle*. Shot partly on the sands and Grand Pier and starring Tommy Trinder in sparkling form at Knightstone, it is a wonderfully nostalgic record of the times.

Meanwhile it was revealed the council had a year earlier bought the Central Cinema prior to redevelopment, which left just the Odeon and Gaumont (as the Regent was re-named in 1954) cinemas in town. The Central was a fleapit but showed what many thought were the best films. Fleapit or no, Knightstone took 500 of its seats at £1 each, half the usual price, but set aside £200 for upholstery repairs.

In 1962 Knightstone's off-season crisis only deepened thanks to awful weather again, that winter going into the record books as one of the century's worst. Reg Dixon, star of *Jack and the Beanstalk,* told its final audience that despite some performances having been cancelled owing to blizzard conditions they had had a wonderful time. Maybe, but the show lost £800, denounced by one councillor as a shocking waste of money, and a council committee decided against any more professional pantomime in Weston, although that decision was reversed.

Aside from pantomime there were only three productions in 1963, during which the theatre closed for 37 weeks, leaving it barely able to meet debt charges from the 1957-8 modernisation and the due share of town hall running costs. More importantly its amenity role was undermined. Landladies complained they couldn't make a living with so short a season: May and September guests bemoaned the lack of evening entertainment and the council was 'doing its best' to drive them away. Amateur groups waded in too, citing their own amenity value to the town and demanding a cut in hire charges. Although Weston Operatic Society had enjoyed its best box office at Easter with *Carousel*, expenses had been heavy and they resented paying £425 for using Knightstone for seven nights, especially as the council raked in a tidy profit from bar takings. Faced with rising production costs the Society hinted at a boycott that would force the council to engage a professional show instead and risk a loss. Society chairman Lew Stuckey stated: 'We are doing them a very good turn and I wish they would realise it.' But the council had overheads too: the theatre's boiler needed replacing at a cost of £6,000; for now, fan heaters would have to do.

Other than its duration, landladies had no reason to complain about the 1963 *Let's Make a Night of It* with Terry Scott and Hugh Lloyd, an outstanding success that broke all box office records. House-full boards were out day after day and the two stars would often provide the celebratory champagne. The show won glowing plaudits – even the Marquess of Bath was a fan – and was fondly remembered for years. Scott, the large, brash

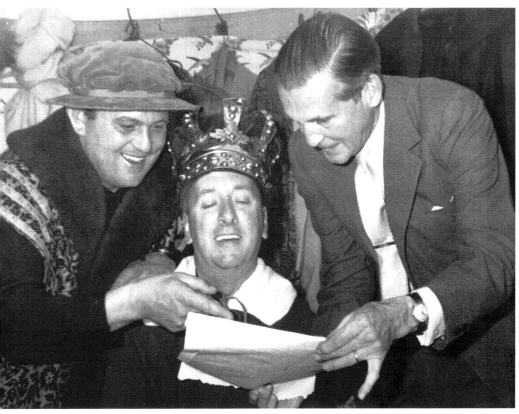

Lord Bath was a fan of Terry Scott and Hugh Lloyd in *Let's Make a Night of It* in 1963. Backstage the pair prepare for a sketch that reversed their usual character roles, Lloyd the dominant King Charles and Scott his harassed messenger.

know-all, and meek and mild Lloyd had a Laurel and Hardy appeal, said the *Mercury*. 'Whoever paired off these two was inspired.' Scott was amusing with his highly expressive face and little boy impersonations while his partner had a nice line in storytelling. Lloyd's wife Jose Stewart sang and played piano. The support cast included Ronald Cryer with marionettes, singer Joe McBride and singer and dancer Terry Fearis. Elsye Monks on organ and Mary Dickie on piano shared the pit with drummer Andrew Reed.

Like many resident stars over the years they immersed themselves in Weston life, Scott moving his Ballet Rambert dancer wife and three young daughters down for the season. Scott and Lloyd judged the Modern Venus competition and met 200 disabled people at Boulevard Congregational

Yvonne Williams operated one of the carbon arc lamps in 1963, shortly before they were replaced with modern spotlights.

Church. They were spotted on the beach and playing tennis. After second house one night in August Charlie Chester, Bert Weedon and Pearl Carr and Teddy Johnson joined them for another BBC *Seaside Night*, the audience invited to stay on for the free entertainment.

Let's Make a Night of It, which like their TV series *Hugh and I* was produced by David Croft, faced strong competition for younger audiences.

The Beatles were live on stage at the Odeon for their legendary week in July, supported by Gerry and the Pacemakers. The Bachelors, Gene Vincent and David Frost with comedian Al Read also starred there during the summer but barely affected one of the best seaside shows of the year. The season ended triumphantly with two gala nights in carnival atmosphere, Scott remarking on stage: 'It has been 12 weeks of absolute Heaven. The women in the box office have been so busy they haven't had time to knit a single sweater.'

But repairs and maintenance devoured show profit: during an unprecedented six-month shutdown that season's £5,000 surplus funded a new telephone switchboard and spotlights to replace the outdated carbon arcs. Just before the closure Bunny Baron had presented a week-long *Those Were the Days* that was tinged with sadness. Part of The Dolly Sisters' act was to bring on two men from the audience to dance the Charleston. One night one of the volunteers collapsed in the wings and was rushed to hospital but later died. His wife said he knew he shouldn't have volunteered as he had a heart condition but he so badly wanted to get up on stage.

The theatre awoke on Easter Saturday 1964 with a sumptuous production of *Showboat* by the Operatic Society, enjoying its sixth decade at Knightstone. After the second war its Savoy operas were a highlight of the entertainment calendar, but by the mid-1950s attendances were down because of television and the draw of American musicals taking Britain by storm. Gilbert and Sullivan was out of fashion – though in truth it had been for many years. Lew Stuckey visited London to check the latest trends, resulting in the Society presenting its first modern musical, the Irving Berlin Broadway hit *Call Me Madam*, in partnership with the Red Triangle Players, in 1956. Doris Foreman of the Society and Leslie Scamp from Red Triangle took the lead roles of Madam (Mrs Sally Adams) and Cosmo Constantine. David Palmer, a young airman from RAF Locking, was given his first chance to tread the boards in the production and a star was born: on leaving the forces he became a principal tenor with the D'Oyly Carte. The show's success changed the mindset of the Society committee, who chose *Oklahoma!* in 1959 and *South Pacific* two years later. But Savoy opera fans were not forgotten: from 1961 the Easter modern musical was complemented with autumn Gilbert and Sullivan, sometimes at the Playhouse. *Call Me Madam* was the first to be produced by Knightstone's former stage manager Wilfred Fredricks, the inspirational driving force behind the

Stagehands in 1963. *Back row*: Mark Jones, George Hastings, Graham Sumner, Mike Newman, Mike Holder, Paul King, Riki Williams, Bob Taylor. *Front row*: Terry Williams, youngster David Brooks, Jane Williams, Lauri Williams, Yvonne Williams, Ray Sum.

Society for more than 30 years. A total of 57 Knightstone shows from 1909 ended with *My Fair Lady* in 1969, after which the Society moved permanently to the Playhouse.

Peter Griffiths, who joined the chorus in 1963, recalled many full houses. 'If you wanted good tickets you had to queue, like the first day of the sales. On the first night of *My Fair Lady* with the Ascot scene we got thunderous applause for just standing there all dressed up. Wilf Fredricks was everything – he designed it, he built it, he produced it. In the autumn show the wind came through and blew the scenery and the backdrops backwards and forwards and it was quite noisy because it was virtually exposed to the elements.'

Lew Stuckey

Tom Shearman

Tom Shearman, the Society's exceptional musical director for 40 years beginning with *Carousel* in 1963, said: 'Backstage was very small, you couldn't fly scenery and the lighting system was pretty outdated by then, but it was a lovely old theatre to play in with lots of wood. Wood's always good for musical instruments – it absorbs. All the pit were in full dress suits with black bow ties – it was always very formal. It began to change from about *The Pajama Game* in 1966 – that was the first really big swinging, slightly jazzy show and I might have worn a white tuxedo for that just to make a difference.'

Steps from stage right led down to four dressing-rooms while steps on the other side descended to one large room, normally for chorus or dancers, and two smaller rooms. Heather Collings, who considered Knightstone a lovely building despite frequent seagull intruders, said: 'Men used the dressing-rooms on one side and women were on the other and never should the two combine. Being a young girl at the time I think they decided that was quite the best idea.'

But another tradition – marathon last-night speeches and presentations – she found tedious and vowed to curtail on becoming Society chairman. 'If you got away under 20 minutes you were doing well. It was like harvest festival. Everyone had flowers and one girl about to be married was given her complete bottom drawer – sheets, pillows, pillow-cases, blankets, the

Ivor Emmanuel, Chris Carlsen and Terry Hall at the 1964 *Let's Make a Night of It* run-through in Hastings. Chris said: 'Hastings were very good to us. They allowed us to make the mistakes, so we ran them in with audiences there like a normal show and made changes before we went to Weston to do the full season'.

lot. There were very long speeches and it wasn't until I took the chairmanship that we stopped thanking the lavatory cleaners. But I got absolutely hauled over the coals at our annual general meeting that I had let the side down.'

Weston-super-Mare Dramatic Society staged two productions a year after the second war and in 1953 became the first amateur group in Britain to present a full-scale version of *Peter Pan*, Jean Jamieson being the first amateur Peter to fly. The Society's future hung in the balance a number of times after poor box offices and financial loss but it nonetheless managed 53 shows at Knightstone over six decades, the last being *Hay Fever* in 1969. The Red Triangle Players, named after the symbol of the YMCA for whom they raised funds, were also Knightstone stalwarts, their casts including Wilf Fredricks, Constance Chapman, Lew Stuckey, Joyce Tidman and, in 1932, Conrad Voss-Bark who became a well-known BBC broadcaster. They had a full-sized orchestra under John J Yates which played before curtain up and during intervals. Other amateurs at Knightstone included the Technical College's College Players, the Alexandra Players and their successors the Wayfarers Drama Group.

After *Showboat* in 1964 the third *Let's Make a Night of It* starred Welsh baritone Ivor Emmanuel whose operatic background set the tone for a show with numbers from *Oklahoma!*, *South Pacific* and other big musicals. 'The stagehands are already calling me Taff,' he told the first-night audience. He was joined in a duet by new wife Patricia Bredin, who in 1957 had been the first UK entrant in the Eurovision Song Contest. Terry Hall with Lenny the Lion and Chris Carlsen provided the comedy. They were essentially soloists who became a knockabout team twice nightly for 12 weeks. Chris recalled: 'In those days the big comedy thing was elephant jokes, such as "How many elephants can you get into a Mini?" We had to make them up and it became a competition. Mine was "What book would an elephant write?" Answer: "An ivory manual". Ivor exploded! It was one of the happiest seasons I have had in my career.' On the last night as the mayor took to the stage to pay tribute, one of the stars, eyeing the full house, drolly remarked: 'Business is looking up at last.'

Throughout August Richard Stone also presented *All-Star Sunday Concerts*, the first of which saw the return of Terry Scott and Hugh Lloyd, who had driven 110 miles from Southsea where they were in a summer show, and most of the cast from their last Knightstone appearance. Lloyd said they had great affection for Weston. Other weeks featured Adam Faith,

Ivor Emmanuel, Patricia Bredin and Terry Hall with Lenny the Lion
pose for a publicity shot in 1964.

Jimmy Clitheroe and Freddie Frinton who stood in at the last moment for an unwell Norman Vaughan. Peter Thorpe, lead guitarist of Adam Faith's backing group The Roulettes, was knocked unconscious on stage by an electric shock caused by a short circuit in his guitar. The group stopped playing and helped carry him to his dressing-room, but by the time an ambulance arrived he had recovered and they completed their performance while he rested.

Chris Carlsen returned three months later as Buttons, with Bob and Alf Pearson as the bill-topping Ugly Sisters, in Bunny Baron's *Cinderella* – but not as originally planned at the Playhouse. In the early hours of Saturday August 22 that theatre was destroyed by fire, caused by a discarded cigarette in the fifth row of the stalls, securing Knightstone's future – though not for long if Basil Flavell had got his way. Weston's catering and entertainments general manager had long wanted to replace Knightstone and the Playhouse with a modern 1,500-seat theatre befitting the town. Three years earlier he had proposed one, together with a conference and banqueting hall, next to the Winter Gardens Pavilion, said to be bursting at the seams. Knightstone would have made way for a competition-standard swimming pool. Now he could barely contain his delight at the loss of the Playhouse as it revived his dream. His son Robert remembers: 'He jumped up and down when the Playhouse burnt down. He wanted the Playhouse and Knightstone replaced with one on the Tivoli site in the Boulevard – that was going to be the ideal. He thought Weston did not justify two theatres. Knightstone was just a drain on resources. But the council wasn't forward-thinking enough.' It re-used the Playhouse's inhibiting site for a replacement less than half the size of the one Mr Flavell had envisaged and there was no talk (yet) of demolishing Knightstone.

Basil Flavell's appointment in 1954 had followed the controversial abolition of the post of director of entertainments and the merger of the catering department, which he had run, with entertainments. The style BH Flavell featured on all Knightstone programmes and posters and he would play a key role in the theatre's fate. Successive employees under him enjoyed the dubious privilege of living in its tower flat as part of the job, to keep it aired as much as anything.

Charles Vance's repertory company lost its scenery and wardrobe in the fire but was bailed out by actors' union Equity and re-housed at the town hall on a makeshift stage. Their season ended at Knightstone with *The Edge of Fear* and *Odd Man In,* punctuated by a Gilbert and Sullivan night with D'Oyly Carte principals Mary Sansom, Gillian Knight, Donald Adams, and David Palmer back on old turf. Amateur companies were offered Knightstone at the Playhouse's lower rates and bookings flooded in from the Red Triangle Players, Wayfarers Drama Group, College Players, Junior Arts Festival, Weston Dramatic Society and, for a second time that year, the

Operatic Society. Injected with new life, Knightstone recuperated from the 37 weeks of closure in 1963 to 28 in 1964, then 19 in each of the next four years until the new Playhouse opened in 1969. This compared with just eight weeks 'in the dark' in 1950 but the world had changed and Knightstone counted its blessings.

It was as well Knightstone hosted *Cinderella* as the cramped old Playhouse would have been a tight squeeze for her glittering crystal coach pulled by Shetland ponies. The animals, stabled near the stage door, were a favourite of Lisa Gaye's girl troupe trained at the Mavdor School of Dancing in Walliscote Grove Road. Pupils from the school, run by Mavis and Doreen James, were an enchanting feature of Knightstone pantomimes for 40 years and over that time the spinster sisters taught different generations of the same families. A dozen girls were chosen at audition for the three-week pantomime, for which they were formally contracted and paid six shillings a week. A Christmas Eve dress rehearsal went on late into the night until producer Bunny Baron was confident of a polished Boxing Day show.

Tansin Benn, then Tansin Shallish, a 12-year-old Mavdor dancer who performed in five consecutive Baron pantomimes, said: 'That rehearsal was stop-start all the time to perfect exits and entrances. It was quite a lot to get right in a theatre with relatively small wings. Being young the dancers often had their parents waiting for them, which was perhaps not so much fun for them.

'Mavis James was the dance teacher while Doreen dealt with the administration and costume support for the Junior Arts Festivals, Eisteddfods and cabarets we were invited to perform in. We had a very disciplined dance training across a range of styles – too strict for some who "jumped" to the Alexander School. They were fun days with plenty of challenges, a time when lifelong friendships were sealed and it left an indelible imprint on all our lives.

'I especially loved the pantomimes where we were contracted and paid as professional dancers. For me the wild, windy walks along the prom to Knightstone in the grey winter days of December and January were all part of the fun. To perform over three weeks every Christmas with a great bunch of what were superstars to us at the time was amazing. I remember we all cried after the "walk-down" at the closing of the last night every year as we said our good-byes.'

Karan Simmons, Tansin Shallish, Len Howe (Dame Trott), Elizabeth Hearne, Jeanette Coles (Red Riding Hood) and Frances Parsons in *Red Riding Hood* in 1965.

Sea-front properties were said to need external redecoration every three years to preserve their appearance, but Knightstone's maintenance budget had been an easy target for savings and now windows were falling out and the weather rushing in. Given its suddenly enhanced status, an urgent £3,000 programme of repairs was authorised.

In 1965 it was like old times, the doors open from the start of April to mid-November, maintaining employment – though most staff were casuals with full-time day jobs. On *Gaytime* and *Let's Make a Night of It* two hands worked stage right, two stage left, there were two flymen, a props man, a chief electrician and two spot operators. Resident shows came with their own wardrobe mistress and stage manager. Lauri Williams, who began as a lime operator in 1957, was by day a Westland Helicopters training officer by the time he left as chief electrician and stage manager in 1979. Like others, he had to be inventive to make Knightstone on time every evening. 'Our attendance did cause a few problems. We would use the excuse that our grandmother had died and we needed to attend the funeral. We had a lot of grandmothers.'

Cabaret Style

Let's Make a Night of It went out in style as a bevy of long-legged showgirls topped with ostrich feathers descended a giant staircase in a glamorous set-piece during the final edition in 1965. Comic Ted Rogers starred with pianist Mrs Mills, folk singers Chas McDevitt and his wife Shirley Douglas – and a Dalek that materialised on stage in a mischievous poke at that deadly rival television.

But Rogers' boundless energy and rapid razor wit could jar with audiences and the atmosphere on VIP first night was decidedly chilly. 'Perhaps he needs to slow down to a more leisurely West Country pace,' advised a press critic. Chas recalled: 'What really upset Ted was the reaction of the dignitaries in the audience – they were all po-faced.' Things got worse at a Winter Gardens banquet where Rogers' temper snapped. 'When they gave a party for the entire cast he went ballistic when he discovered they had cut up the box office poster to make the table place names and that people should sit in the room according to their billing. Ted went round and changed all the placings, allowing dancers to sit on the top table, etcetera.'

Those official functions for Knightstone and Playhouse casts (when the Playhouse was open) contrasted with less-formal buffets in the Knightstone bar on opening and closing nights of *Gaytime* and *Let's Make a Night of It,* hosted by the mayor for cast, crew and front-of-house staff – the council entertainments committee never slow to tuck in. Such hospitality fell victim to cuts in the mid-1960s but cast and stagehands continued to toast end-of-seasons at lock-ins in a local bar. Rogers, who arranged a farewell do of his own at the Grand Atlantic Hotel where he was staying, had fixed up a television in his dressing-room for the 12-week run, perhaps to refresh his satirical take on TV commercials. Mrs Mills gave the show a homely quality with her dry Cockney wit – if not the washing machine she had installed in *her* dressing-room!

A less-edgy humour from Norman Vaughan, who had recently risen to fame hosting *Sunday Night at the London Palladium*, followed in 1966. He had heard such a glowing account from Terry Scott of his time in Weston that he was determined to try it for himself and with Richard Stone jointly produced the twice-nightly, 12-week *Norman Vaughan Show*. Vaughan was

The Promenade and Knightstone Causeway, Weston-super-Mare. ET.4112R

A postcard shows a busy Knightstone during the 1965 run of *Let's Make a Night of It.*

in great form, singing, dancing and cracking jokes in his inimitable style and working with children without letting them steal the show, said a review. Comedy magician Frankie Holmes was a popular co-star who borrowed three mice to use in his act and without any magic soon had eight with more on the way. Instead of the usual band in the pit, one of Britain's top saxophonists, Betty Smith, led a quintet which displayed great verve and skill – but sometimes drowned out the singers! Although not a good year for summer shows because of strained finances, it was seen by 55,000 and judged one of the best.

It was a different story for that year's *Aladdin,* with Arthur English as Widow Twankey, which suffered a poor box office and bruising *Mercury* verdict. 'To drag children away from the less costly attractions of Napoleon Solo and Lady Penelope needs more enterprise than this, despite what parents say about the magic of pantomime as they nostalgically remember it.' Some readers thought the criticism unduly harsh, especially as children

Anthony Menary (Emperor), Shirley May (Princess) and Lisa Gaye's
dancers in *Aladdin* in 1966.

had loved Don Maclean's Wishee Washee, and the chairman of the entertainments committee sprung to the show's defence, insisting, somewhat
generously, it had been one of the best pantomimes the town had seen. It
was more proof the public was not prepared to leave the comfort of their
homes, and now three television channels, in winter for actors they had
barely heard of.

Two of Knightstone's longest-running shows were the 16-week summer
seasons in 1967 and 1968 of *The Fol-de-Rols*, an irreverent revue with a
pedigree dating back to 1911 in Scarborough, where it had begun as an

Harry Corbett and Sooty starred in one-night fund-raisers for the National Children's Home organisation in 1954 and 1955, and *The Sooty Talent Show* in 1967, a three-day try-out before a London theatre Christmas. They returned with Sweep, Soo and Ramsbottom in 1968 for this prematurely titled follow-up.

indoor successor to a beach pierrot show. The first season, headlined by comedian Freddie Sales and vocalist Jennifer Toye, a former D'Oyly Carte principal, was reviewed as 'racy and vivacious' and 'right up to the Beatling moment'. Knightstone needed good winter and poor summer weather to haul in the crowds and high temperatures that year kept tourists out of doors, turning a predicted £2,200 profit into a £200 loss. Once again the council found itself on the defensive, but even as Mr Flavell praised it as 'a universally accepted show which could not be bettered' he was plotting sweeping changes to his entertainment venues in the name of modernisation that would mean nothing less than the end of Knightstone as a traditional theatre. The stalls were to be replaced with tables and chairs and waiter service, a move struggling theatres were copying from the London Hippodrome which had become theatre-restaurant The Talk of the Town in 1958. Such a cabaret club-style arrangement was surely no place for pantomime, drama or opera, so it seemed Knightstone was destined to host summer seasons only. At the same time the side of the theatre facing Marine Lake was to get a new look. The box office and Harbour Café would be replaced with a Harbour Bar, restaurant and 'continental' terrace dining, to the fury of a local publican who accused the council of muscling in on his business. The existing bar was to become the new box office. Mr Flavell said the theatre had been built as a ballroom pavilion and was not up to current standards. All types of show had been tried and there was a point below which they could not drop. Holidaymakers were no longer captive customers – the young were more affluent, had cars and used Weston as a touring base. 'Second rate in any form of entertainment is no longer acceptable.'

Little public comment greeted the proposals. Everyone was preoccupied in opposition to his plan to turn Rozel bandstand into a games centre and move Vernon Adcock's bandshow to the Winter Gardens. Their objections partly succeeded: Adcock was relocated but the bandstand was revamped as Rozel Sun Lounge and Café with light music, organ and Sunday bands. These 'modernisations' did not satisfy Weston and District Ratepayers' and Residents' Association which wanted the entire catering and entertainment department privatised as losses at Knightstone, Marine Lake, the Winter Gardens and Rozel now amounted to a 3d rate. Flavell had always opposed leasing out the theatre, arguing that the best people were hired to stage shows while the council operated the building, which in his view it could do better than anyone else. He was thus equally opposed to privatisation, insisting there would be no takers as they would first have to stump up £7,000 on annual overheads at Knightstone alone. The Association would have to wait 23 years for legislation compelling councils to 'privatise' their leisure venues.

The first production of 1968 was blighted by tragedy when eminent musical director William Cox-Ife was killed in an air crash hours before he was due as guest conductor and piano accompanist at a Gilbert and Sullivan for All Sunday concert with D'Oyly Carte soloists Valerie Masterton, Donald Adams, Phillip Potter and Helen Landis. In the finest tradition of 'the show must go on' frantic arrangements were made to fill his dual role. At 4pm Weston Operatic Society accompanist Jessica Hillman, who was planning to see the concert, received a phone call request to cover for Mr Cox-Ife on piano despite many of the numbers being new to her. After a brief rehearsal she had 15 minutes to hurry back home to change, leaving no time to put on make-up. The Society's musical director Tom Shearman stepped in as conductor and an announcement was made about the changes without giving the reason so as not to affect the audience's enjoyment. Mrs Hillman's superb ability to sight-read, enabling her to play at concert standard from a strange score, saved the day and both she and Mr Shearman received an ovation from audience, soloists and chorus. It was the first time Mrs Hillman had taken a bow from the Knightstone stage in her long association with the theatre. Modestly she said later it had been a thrill and a privilege to accompany such great artistes.

The council considered it vital that the new Playhouse made a good first impression when it opened in July 1969, but with top stars charging £1,000 a week and entertainment costs already high a tough choice had to be made. It controversially decided to focus resources on a Playhouse summer show with television personality while Knightstone would have to make do with repertory. Critics pointed out the Playhouse was intended for repertory and amateur dramatics and that its limited 686-seat capacity could never recoup the cost of such a glitzy production. The 950-seat Knightstone, on the other hand, was ideally suited and placed for summer revue so repertory there would be inappropriate and wasteful. 'Theatrical Madness' screamed a *Mercury* headline. Some suggested, not entirely flippantly, they may as well fill Knightstone with slot machines or a casino if they really wanted it to pay its way. John Redgrave, who had climbed the profession from Knightstone props hand to leading show producer, put it bluntly: 'The butcher and baker wanted to serve on the entertainments committee but didn't have a clue about running theatres.' The decision was overturned on discovery that such a Playhouse show would indeed not pay for itself. Instead it would open, appropriately enough, with a Brian Rix farce while Sandy Powell fronted old-time music hall at Knightstone.

The different genres no longer welcome at Knightstone took their farewell bows, some less auspiciously than others, as the great exodus to the Playhouse began. The last pantomime, *Robin Hood and his Merry Men*, which opened on Boxing Day 1968 with no star names, was an undistinguished finale to a formidable tradition. By contrast, the amateurs went out in style. The Operatic Society's *My Fair Lady* at Easter 1969 was its most

My Fair Lady, Weston Operatic Society's spectacular last production
at Knightstone in 1969.

Brynley James, Stan Bailey
and Peter Brewer in the 1969
My Fair Lady.

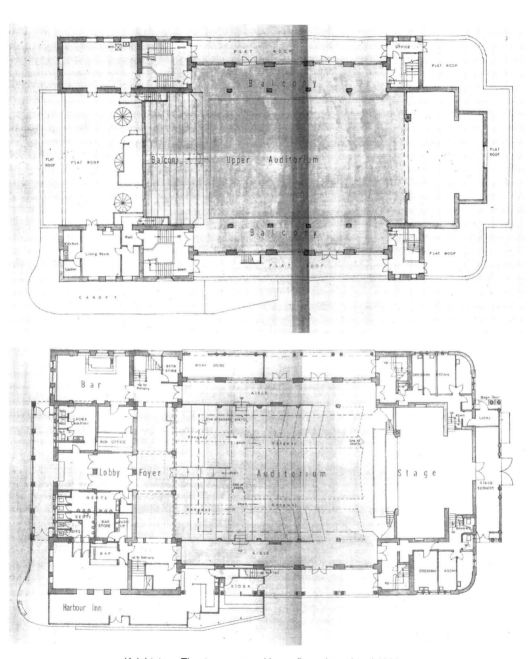

Knightstone Theatre upper and lower floor plans dated 1966.

ambitious venture yet. A top London costumier created the wardrobe for a cast of 60, the orchestra was augmented and helpers made more than 1,000 paper flowers for the colourful Covent Garden market scene. The mayor and mayoress, heads of neighbouring towns and the Bishop of Bath and Wells attended a special civic night and all eight performances sold out. Others followed on, culminating with the Wayfarers' production of *Quiet Weekend,* the last performance of which on May 17 brought down the curtain on 60 years of amateur productions.

The next to leave was repertory, the honour going appropriately to Charles Vance's company. Vance was the last of the old-time actor-managers, a raffish character who might be seen in green velvet jacket brandishing a silver-topped cane once owned by his hero Henry Irving. Vance alone had appeared in *Son of Oblomov* with Bill Kerr and Valerie van Ost in 1966. His company, Knightstone regulars since the Playhouse fire, included future television stars John Inman and Sue Nicholls. It left in style too, with guest character actor Valentine Dyall in *The Edge of Fear,* which ended on June 7.

Workmen then had four days to transform the theatre into a Victorian music hall setting for summer show *Let's All Go to the Music Hall.* Some rows of stalls seating were replaced with tables and chairs for a drinks-only waiter service. The bright blue auditorium was repainted a traditional theatrical crimson, and fairy lights framed the proscenium. This severely reduced capacity from 950 to 650, ironically leaving fewer seats than at the Playhouse recently deemed too small for expensive productions. But it was some way short of a full conversion to cabaret club style, which would not happen for another six years.

Several councillors considered a nostalgia show inappropriate for holiday crowds, but the high-quality bill of stars with long and distinguished careers in showbusiness proved a hit, and surprisingly with a large number of youngsters. Veteran comic Sandy Powell brought the house down with his cod ventriloquism act and genial line in gags. He co-starred with statuesque queen of music hall singers Margery Manners, impressionist Peter Cavanagh and Irish tenor Cavan O'Connor, the 'Strolling Vagabond of Song'. Top-hatted and moustachioed Eddie Reindeer looked the part of Victorian master of ceremonies with his own table and gavel. It was spoilt only by backstage squabbles between 69-year-old Powell and 70-year-old O'Connor over which of them was top of the bill.

Table seats at 10s 6d and normal stalls at 7s 6d helped receipts initially buck the depressing downward trend at other resorts, but the 15-week run ended £6,000 below estimate and the council promised a more conventional entertainment for 1970. In fairness the show had faced keen competition from the new £230,000 Playhouse, now with balcony, which opened with Brian Rix and Leo Franklyn in *Let Sleeping Wives Lie*. Leslie Crowther took over from Rix a month later. At a Red Triangle Players dinner Basil Flavell left no doubt about council priorities. Running theatres was expensive and if there was to be a subsidy it would be for the Playhouse, whose diary for the first year was virtually full. Knightstone had been 'a stumbling block since 1901', but he predicted it might even contribute financially to the Playhouse if plans for it were successful.

In the 1970s Knightstone presented a summer show only. The theatre was locked up for nine months of most years of the decade, but when the holiday season came round it burst into life with Bunny Baron's *Summer Showboat,* nightly at eight with a programme change on Thursdays. The 1970 headliner was singer Tony Mercer from *The Black and White Minstrel Show,* who had first appeared at Knightstone in a 1948 ex-forces show packed with down-to-earth humour. His richly resonant voice carried old-time numbers around the auditorium, then he sat at a mirror and 'blacked up' leisurely on stage as he recounted tales of his television career before leading everyone in a selection of Al Jolson favourites. Comedian Alton Douglas and magician Roy Earl exploited the new layout to involve the audience in their acts. The 13-week show attracted capacity crowds, who enjoyed the table service that cut out the usual mad scamper to the bar in the interval.

Income was up on forecasts, but soaring inflation, and patronage so unexpectedly dire at the Playhouse they began showing films, threatened to send the entertainments charge on Weston's rates crashing through the £56,000 legal limit. There was even talk of saving £1,700 by calling time on the famous floral clock, which in 1935 had replaced the World War One tank in Alexandra Gardens. Another institution, the Modern Venus competition, also looked doomed, one official branding it a 'failing event' for which girls had to be virtually kidnapped to enter. To boost income Knightstone was let to a bingo operator for 17 months despite objections to gambling on council premises, bingo being suspended for the 1971 show. The move was popular and punters petitioned for a permanent conversion,

Comic Sandy Powell in white tuxedo headed the bill in *Let's all Go to the Music Hall* in 1969. Eddie Reindeer was the top-hatted chairman.

but the council stressed its commitment to a summer show. That left a market which the Rank Organisation tapped two years later when it turned the Gaumont, a cinema for 60 years, into a Top Rank Bingo and Social Club.

As long as it went on attracting high-profile performers *Summer Showboat* could keep afloat. This it did in style in 1971 with husband and wife singers Pearl Carr and Teddy Johnson in an ideal production for Weston, being 'wrapped in gorgeous colours and dressings' and including much audience participation. Pearl and Teddy were well known after coming second in the 1959 Eurovision Song Contest with *Sing, Little Birdie* and for appearances on light entertainment television programmes. They

Tables and waiter service gave the theatre a cabaret club feel.

were joined by conjurer-comedian Frankie Holmes, back for a third visit, and comedy dancers Martin and Sylvia Konyot. Bookings poured in, including a party of 130 from a Swindon factory and a group of 157 from a local caravan site. Pearl had announced she would retire from show business at the end of the season but enjoyed herself so much that she decided to carry on.

Few top television stars would now commit to a resident show, and Knightstone could scarcely afford those who did. The headliners in following years were less famous, if not unknown – West End musicals singer Barry Kent, comedian Derek Roy from radio's *Variety Bandbox* in the 1950s and comedian Bobby Dennis. A reviewer urged producers to re-think the show's style. 'Some of the *Showboat* programme is better suited to a darkened auditorium and a strong spotlight than to the half-light provided by the coloured bulbs strung from the balcony.'

A local government reorganisation added to the theatre's insecurity, as surrounding areas in the new 'Woodspring' would have to foot Weston entertainment losses for the first time – and the incoming council didn't entirely approve of how the money was being spent. While the 1974 bill-topper was harmless 1940s radio singer and comedian Reg Dixon, councillors in the best seats on first night were alarmed at the sight of 24-year-old pop star Barry Hopkins. He recalled: 'My billing was Barry Hopkins – Bright and Breezy and some years later I asked the then entertainments director why I had never been invited back. To my utter horror evidently some of the councillors thought I was on speed as I had so much energy on stage!'

Dixon, a burly figure in trilby hat whose catchphrase was 'I'm not well, I'm proper poorly', had an intimate manner, reflected in the homeliness of his dressing-room, proudly adorned with pictures of him with Prince Philip, Maurice Chevalier and Laurel and Hardy. Musical clown Ravel, whose fractured English gave the show an international flavour, was in fact the son of a Dutchman who came from Weston. Otherwise Alfred Vorzanger, he was joined by his wife, comedienne and singer Bonnie Downs.

Actually, Woodspring was beneficial, initially anyway. Basil Flavell, now as its director of leisure services, fully converted the theatre to cabaret style, replacing the remaining stalls seats with tables and chairs. An apron was built over the pit, and the musicians – down to three or four – played at the back of the stage. Weston favourites Pearl Carr and Teddy Johnson were brought back in an appropriately re-titled *Cabaret Showtime* for 1975. Pearl noticed the difference from their last visit, remarking: 'The foyer and bar are different but the atmosphere remains. There's a nice feeling about this theatre – a feeling I haven't had anywhere else. It's rather like a large club now – relaxed, informal and intimate and the sort of entertainment we are staging fits perfectly.' The couple were very fond of Weston but their plans to settle permanently in the resort fell through. The show was seen by 30,000 and but for exceptionally good weather would have broken summer records.

Dai Francis starred in 1976, very much in the style of fellow *Black and White Minstrel Show* soloist Tony Mercer six years earlier. The Welsh bass-baritone sang subdued, almost sombre, numbers before donning Al Jolson face, and, with flashing eyes, poured out the sentimental ballads all had come to hear. Lauri Williams saw it from a slightly different backstage perspective: 'As top of the bill he would turn up in the interval, apply his make-up on stage in front of the audience to do his act and be out of the theatre almost before they had got out of their seats and down to the police social club.'

The season had been profitable but during the building's deep hibernations only basic maintenance was carried out – even a hand on the theatre clock was still missing after two years. Knightstone could no longer live off its summers and in a surprise move Woodspring proposed its conversion to a bowling centre. Equally surprising, the imminent end of live entertainment after three-quarters of a century sparked not a murmur of protest, a £233,000 plan to modernise the adjacent baths grabbing all the attention. There was greater concern that garish theatre advertising boards had sprung up along the front and were lowering the tone.

There was still time to squeeze in a few more summer seasons, but those shows were desperate throwbacks to a lost world of variety, without the redemption of star names. The 1977 headliners were ex-miners Millican and Nesbitt, whose dated act was close-harmony country and western songs with everyone expected to join in. And when the year after little more than half the seats were sold for obscure Spanish singers Los Zafiros, comics The Patton Brothers and illusionists Van Buren and Greta, Knightstone's future returned to the agenda. Now it was to be a sports centre with bowling greens, billiards, table tennis and skittle alley, compensated for by extended seasons at the Playhouse and Winter Gardens where ticket sales had been equally grim.

Basil Flavell said the economics of them all were beginning to give him 'considerable concern'. That was barely-concealed code for Weston being in deep trouble, having failed to keep pace with modern holiday trends. Some hotels had become convalescent homes or holiday flats and an increasing number of pubs, fully licensed guest houses and hotels with colour television were competing with theatregoing. He accepted he was closing a theatre while serving on a national committee campaigning to keep them open but airily dismissed it as 'a pavilion over a water tank, unsuitable for anything'. The *Mercury* demanded a thorough re-examination of the town's entertainments, asking 'Are we really offering the bulk of

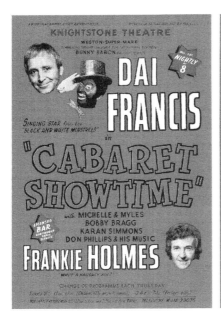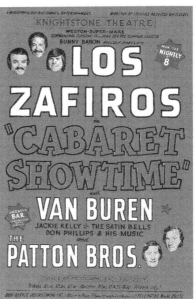

Dai Francis and Los Zafiros were *Cabaret Showtime* headliners
in 1976 and 1978 respectively.

today's visitors what they want or are we persisting with a formula that
certainly used to pack them in but now suddenly seems precariously dated?'
Brian Austin, a local historian and former professional actor, given the job
of painting Knightstone's backstage areas, suspected it had been deliberately
run down to get beyond saving. 'I was ordered to use soft brushes so as not
to break the seal that held the powdered plaster in. Not long after that a hand
dropped a stage brace against the back wall and caused a landslide of
powder that had to be removed in a cart.'

But as Knightstone's closure loomed, the town belatedly woke up to the
implications. Potential visitors were already going further south and it was
feared many more would do so if the theatre were lost. What a short time
ago was being blamed for Weston's out-datedness was now hailed as its
saviour. The Hotels' and Restaurants' Association and Weston and
Woodspring Ratepayers' Association, while happy with an out-of-season
sports centre, demanded retention of the summer show. Two thousand
signed a petition against closure and the Upper Church Road Traders'

Len Lowe, Bobby Crush, theatre manager Les Smith and Bernie Clifton enjoy a full house in 1979.

Association, worried their businesses would suffer, placed a protest notice in the *Mercury*. Even a march was organised, but was called off at the last moment after intervention from Bunny Baron, anxious not to rock the boat as he was still engaged by Woodspring elsewhere. Flavell explained that Knightstone could never again operate all year as a theatre because sparse off-seasons would deter artistes, and seating could not be re-installed for summer shows once bowling greens had been laid down. But councillors, yielding to the groundswell of anger, conceded that even the best theatres had to be subsidised. They threw out the conversion scheme and approved live entertainment for 1979.

Sadly those arrangements were plunged into doubt with the death of Bunny Baron. A former East End boy actor, he had had a golden touch when it came to holiday resorts and brought a host of household names to Weston. His choreographer wife Lisa Gaye, whose dance troupes had been charming features of Knightstone pantomimes, still ran their productions company and came to the rescue. But it would be her last year in the role so the reprieve was temporary and the three-month *Bernie Clifton Show* was the last traditional revue at Knightstone. It was a worthy finale with tremendous box office.

Comic Bernie Clifton posed for the press next to a house-full sign and urged the town to save the theatre: 'Knightstone is a nice theatre to work in and I hope it doesn't close. Too many theatres are dying. It would be nice to see the local residents make a stand to keep the Knightstone.' He rode Oswald the ostrich, telling enthralled children he found the egg in a theatre fire bucket. Pianist Bobby Crush co-starred with dwarf Rusty Goffe, comedian Len Lowe and Lisa Gaye's dancers.

There were two shows, changing on Thursdays, but really every night was different thanks to improvisation – which didn't always work. Bernie recalled: 'Len knew every comedy sketch in the book and what we didn't use from his archive we invented. Bobby and I wrote a parody on the Village People who were huge at the time. Bobby would sit at the piano playing a medley of their hits but dressed as a very old lady whilst I would vocalise dressed as an elderly army colonel – all clothes bought at various village fetes we attended. The problem was, we decided to perform it during the interval without telling the management. So the curtains closed at the end of the first half, to open a minute later to the sight and sound of me and the Crush. The audience, who had just got to the bar, promptly returned to their seats. Our five-minute routine ended in silence, and if that wasn't bad enough we were told the bar takings were down by over £100. We were mortified, although it had seemed like a good idea at the time.'

Undaunted, the popularity of film *Watership Down* gave Bernie the idea of borrowing a large fluffy rabbit from a neighbour of his rented bungalow in Hutton for use in an act. 'I invited a youngster from the audience to join me on stage, sat him down and gave him the rabbit to cuddle while I sang *Bright Eyes*. The rabbit panicked and virtually shredded the lad's smart Fair Isle pullover. A disaster. Never again! Returning the bunny to his hutch that night I said to him: "That was your big chance and you blew it".'

Bernie also recalled the night assistant stage manager Bernie Watts, a member of Weston's lifeboat crew, was summoned in the middle of a show. 'At the end of one scene the curtains didn't close as they should have. We looked in the wings, no sign of Bernard, just the rope swinging in the breeze. The lifeboat warning had gone and he had dropped everything and, getting his priorities right, headed for the slipway. We managed fine.'

Len Lowe, who also produced the show, attributed its success to freshness and spontaneity and reported that one family had travelled down from London four times just to see it. 'If people come that far, the show must be a winner. Shows are being cancelled in Devon and Cornwall but this one is getting better each night.' But while the 35,000 audience total beat the Playhouse's bedroom farces, it didn't avert another annual loss, and with inevitably costlier productions in 1980 Woodspring worried that average families were unlikely to fork out £2 a person to shelter in a theatre in bad weather.

Weston was at a crossroads and had to choose between two distinct routes ahead. On one hand, an English Tourist Board study revealed the industry was worth £24 million to the local economy, justifying substantially more council investment than the current £300,000. It deplored the 'dereliction' of some amenities and proposed a five-year action plan to breathe new life into The Pool, Marine Lake and Birnbeck Pier.

On the other, Roger Harris, Woodspring's economic development chairman, argued Weston had too many sacred cows, like Knightstone, which was on a prime site but used just 14 weeks a year and only then for three hours a day. The council could no longer pump money into out-of-date venues – it only added to their losses and they were still left with old buildings. Besides, council borrowing was being curbed. Others warned against talking Weston down but agreed the town was drab and down-at-heel. The Hotels' and Restaurants' Association predicted a 'day of reckoning' as most of the town's major amenities dated from before the war and now needed a lot more than just a lick of paint. The general mood was for private investment to reinvigorate the resort, but not with arcades of slot machines: Blackpool it was not.

No strategic decisions had been taken by 1980 so some rather deft scheduling was called for now the era of variety and revue was well and truly over. Vernon Adcock and his eight-piece orchestra, looking forward to their record 26th Weston season, were transferred from the Winter Gardens to present a three-month entertainment that changed mid-week from music show with guest pianist Semprini, who had first appeared at Knightstone in 1950, to good-old-days sing-song. Vernon welcomed the move – the haphazard acoustics of the Winter Gardens ballroom could bounce music back at him from three different directions. Knightstone, though larger, was a more intimate setting for his sweet melodies of Cole Porter, George Gersh-

The 1980 Vernon Adcock Show featured singers Christine Campbell,
Suzy Brown, Peter Lewis and Roger Green.

win and Jerome Kern. Traditional stalls seating was re-introduced, suiting
his elderly fans who turned out in greater numbers than ever. Remarkably,
it was a theatre again. A novel series of Sunday evening concerts featured
some of Britain's best brass bands.

The next year Vernon was joined by Canadian tenor John Hanson but cut-
backs put paid to any star guest in his third and last Knightstone season. So
after another nine-month closure the theatre re-opened in June 1982 to *Vernon
Adcock's Wonderful World of Music* with just regular singers Christine
Campbell, Peter Lewis and Karl Rainer. Two hours of pure nostalgia included
I've Got a Lovely Bunch of Coconuts and *There'll Always be an England* with
giant song sheets, and when a huge Union Jack appeared as a backdrop for a
selection of World War Two favourites it was greeted in the patriotic mood
generated by the recent Falklands War with spontaneous applause. Christine,
who dazzled in frequently changed gowns from a wardrobe of 30 that
included her 19-year-old wedding dress now coloured mauve and studded
with sequins, revealed that many holidaymakers spent every evening at the
show – and even asked why they didn't perform on Sundays!

Clive Jackson in the new combined post of leisure and tourism director

Traditional stalls seating was re-introduced for Vernon Adcock's shows.
Above: The stage is set for the 1981 season,
below: Some tables remain at the back.

The poorly lit foyer in 1981 with refreshment area and notice banning use of cameras.

reported a disappointing season, the World Cup, Wimbledon and Falklands conflict having kept many in front of their televisions. Vernon's show had not been immune, attracting an average audience of just 290 in a theatre that could now seat 711. Worse, urgent upgrades totalling £100,000 were needed, including a new heating system to prevent a build-up of condensation in the closed months that had caused an outbreak of fungus in the west tower, which had had to be sealed off.

Everyone had their own ideas for the building. Council officers proposed its conversion to all-year community and tourist use. The Civic Society and Chamber of Trade came up with a bitty scheme, fashionable at the time, of a 'mini Covent Garden' of arts and crafts stalls, exhibition space and studio theatre. Councillors wanted the town museum moved in, infuriating its staff. Just as the theatre looked truly doomed it was saved yet again by disaster, as it had been by the fires at the Grand Pier in 1930 and Playhouse in 1964. Rozel Café, the pleasant suntrap where visitors relaxed in deckchairs to the sounds of a Hammond organ or Weston Concert Band, had to be demolished following irreparable damage to Marine Lake colonnade in a night of ferocious gales and tidal surge in December 1981. At first this gentle entertainment was to be moved to the Tropicana Pleasure Beach, which had recently replaced The Pool, the classic 1937 lido where Modern Venus contestants had been judged by many a Knightstone star. But the Hotels' and Restaurants' Association doubted whether older guests staying in the Knightstone area would trudge half-a-mile to the Tropicana and imagined they would be horrified by its boisterous crowds and blaring transistors if they did. If both Knightstone and Rozel closed there would be little left for the town's most loyal clientele.

The point was well made and in May 1983 the theatre won a new lease of life with the surprise name of The Knightstone Centre. The traditional seating had been removed again and an organ installed for an 18-week season called *The Organist Entertains,* in which John King played for two hours at noon and 8pm daily. It lacked Rozel's atmosphere but was not weather dependent and enjoyed such popularity the run was extended by a month. Roller-disco sessions were held between his appearances. The integral Harbour Inn was smartly refurbished and its beer supplier Courage sponsored an exhibition snooker night starring world champion Steve Davis, 40 years after an earlier world champion, Joe Davis, had played exhibition snooker under the same roof. For the 1984 season the council provided a new Hammond Commodore organ and Friday evenings sold out. A huge scooter rally descended on Weston in mid-September, and while there were disturbances in town, a non-alcoholic all-night disco at Knightstone passed off peacefully.

Karl Rainer, the singer in Vernon Adcock's show, now back at the Winter Gardens with its limited staging and lighting effects, regretted the loss of Knightstone as a traditional theatre, saying he missed it tremendously. 'I feel it is the only legitimate theatre in Weston. The Playhouse is all right, but you cannot replace the character and authenticity of Knightstone.'

Knightstone was still closed for most of the year and Woodspring viewed its makeover as a stopgap measure that didn't solve the dilemma of long-term viability. It produced a glossy marketing brochure inviting redevelopment of the entire peninsula, if necessary demolishing all buildings, despite their being in a conservation area, and filling in part of Marine Lake for car parking. 'We must chuck a few of the sacred cows overboard,' said one councillor. Another, John Crockford-Hawley, dismissed The Centre as 'a glorified church hall with a ghastly electronic organ at the end'. Resident organist Alan Cox responded by playing a hymn to his audience, who 'fell about laughing'.

The Civic Society was outraged at the prospect of demolition and wondered 'how long are these people going to go on destroying Weston's character and viability as a resort?' The town was stuck at the bottom end of the holiday market and its Victorian character should be better protected. The press was deluged with protest letters. One claimed that not long ago the council had wanted to demolish the Winter Gardens Pavilion and Italian Gardens and now these 'Philistines' were turning on another heritage landmark. The Tropicana, a purgatory of noise and tastelessness, was seen as a portent of the future. Marine Lake was the one place the tide stayed in: replace it with car parking and Weston was finished. The strength of feeling was reflected in the size of a petition, signed by 22,000 people, including 16 schools that used Knightstone baths.

The council's submission to an English Tourist Board report called Resorts 2000 revealed its radical thinking. It wanted to change the town's identity to an events centre for walking, riding, golf, caving, sailing, wind-surfing and water-skiing. Weston's time-honoured image as a bucket-and-spade resort would not be abandoned but to rely on a 'limited unfashionable product' would lead to 'a spiral of decline'.

As the row raged on, Courage put The Centre on a sounder footing by introducing all-year use. After *The Organist Entertains* and dance sessions in summer it stayed open off-season for pool, snooker, darts and skittles, but roller-skating was discontinued. In return for its £75,000 investment the company's liquor contract was extended by five years. Steve Davis returned in July 1986 to officially re-open the premises, which now had longer hours of 10am to 11pm. At the same time he opened an extended boat slipway and got stuck in the mud.

Courage's initiative was a blessing, for the attempt to market the peninsula failed abysmally. Although 60 potential investors had been shown round the site, only one detailed, and rather bizarre, scheme was forthcoming and was flatly rejected. This was submitted by a local resident who wanted to raise the Marine Lake breakwater by 11ft, create a cascade and place holiday huts on a new causeway. Clive Jackson said developers had been put off by the lack of car parking space and the corrosive effect of the sea.

Despite much activity already going on, unexpectedly from December 1986 the Centre also became a pop concert venue, hosting an impressive line-up of stars including Georgie Fame and the Blue Flames, Steve

Marriott, George Melly, The Tremeloes, The Searchers, The Sweet, Geno Washington and the Ram Jam Band and Desmond Dekker and the Aces. Geno Washington was brought back by public demand after a sell-out performance. Mr Jackson hoped Knightstone would become as established a home for live music as the Winter Gardens had been in the 1960s and 1970s. The concerts were so popular that three had to be cancelled while the bar was extended from 6ft to 30ft. Alcohol-fuelled scuffles broke out during Desmond Dekker's appearance but fears that the concerts would be stopped because of the prospect of drunken rowdiness proved groundless.

By sharp contrast, genteel afternoon tea dances attracted parties from far and wide thanks to the standing of hosts Ted and Sue Burroughs and the appeal of a day in Weston. Sue recalled: 'We used to get full coachloads from Birmingham, Wales and Cornwall. It was a special day out for them. They would have a little bit of time around town, come to the tea dance and have a fish and chip supper before going home. It was much nicer to come to a ballroom rather than their church hall.' Ted and Sue would lead off sequence dances, to CD or record accompaniment.

Knightstone Singers' and Dancers' Club met on Sunday evenings and the Centre found room for more sports, including archery and table tennis. Even drama returned, with a performance by newly formed TOPPS Drama Club of Leslie Sands' *Beside the Seaside*, about the bad old days of 1950s seaside boarding houses.

So with organ music, pop concerts, sport sessions, tea and ballroom dancing, ad-hoc bookings such as a toy fair, and the ever-present pool, snooker, darts and skittles, the old place began to enjoy a real renaissance.

Dilapidation

That internal rebirth was oblivious to the building's external decay. In April 1989 pictures splashed across the *Mercury* revealed a crumbling balustrade, rusting ironwork and overall dirty and shoddy appearance. 'Shameful neglect' one of many appalled readers put it. Another small fortune would have to be found to keep the Centre open. There was talk of re-marketing the peninsula but the cost of just doing that was high and, of course, the last attempt had failed.

Fortunately several developers came forward and were encouraged to submit formal schemes. Tycoon Peter de Savary, already planning a £250 million leisure and industrial park at Weston airfield, envisaged a 280-bedroom hotel, shops accessible from the beach and underground parking. Another company wanted to convert the Centre to a 50-bedroom 'health' hotel and keep only the pool façade. But a developer who pledged £2.5 million to save and enhance all the buildings perhaps unsurprisingly got the go-ahead. Kingfisher Leisure aimed to turn the Centre into a discotheque, revamp the pool and convert Dr Fox's Georgian bath-house into a restaurant. The buildings would be linked by covered walkways and in American style porters would park cars in what was currently the underground settling tank. The company was granted a management contract to run the peninsula pending a 125-year lease.

For a while things looked up for Weston. A large Tesco store had opened on an old railway goods yard, work had begun on a better road out to the M5 and preparations were in hand for the £30 million Sovereign Shopping Centre. The Winter Gardens Pavilion was to be refurbished and its rear Starlight Room replaced with a conference centre that would attract more staying visitors. Some bookings were transferred to Knightstone during that 18-month contract. Two swimming pools were planned for Hutton Moor Leisure Centre, the Odeon was getting a fourth screen and Peter de Savary's airfield Europark promised 4,000 jobs.

But by the end of 1989 the first snag hit Kingfisher's scheme. At a licensing hearing a nightclub objected to the proposed discotheque, and at another the police opposed any late opening because it could overstretch them. The council came to the rescue by applying for the required permission on its

Roller-skating sessions were held during the 1983 and 1984 summers.

own public entertainments licence and transferring that permission to the company. By then it was too late to begin conversion work before the 1990 summer so Kingfisher put everything on hold and laid on a lavish entertainment programme with the accent on nostalgia, re-branding the Centre as Knightstone Showbar, a most unexpected of revivals.

Hoteliers and a civic party were invited to the opening production, *That'll be the Day*, a celebration of rock-and-roll through the decades, which became a weekly fixture, as did wrestling, comedy shows and Sixties nights with well-known groups. The highlight was *Summer Showtime* on Fridays with guests including The Wurzels, The Mad Hatters and The Brother Lees. The daytime organist disappeared as did Knightstone Singers' and Dancers' Club but their Sunday slot was taken by ballroom dancing with organist from the closed Winter Gardens.

All seemed to be going well until a new hitch scuppered Kingfisher's entire plan. The company wanted to move Weston Bay Yacht Club into the bath-house so its wooden clubhouse could be replaced with a glazed sun terrace. But the club, a Knightstone tenant since 1932, could not afford the higher rent and likely £30,000 bill to fit out its proposed new home, so insisted on staying put for the remaining seven years of its lease unless the matter could be resolved. After some acrimony the company broke off talks and was faced with having to start again with a new planning application that excluded the clubhouse. It was not willing to commit more funds and in December 1990 pulled out, handing peninsula control back to the council.

Suddenly Weston's optimism of only a few months earlier evaporated. Just as Knightstone, with its perpetual maintenance bill, returned to haunt the local authority so Peter de Savary's Europark scheme spectacularly collapsed. Dozens of bulbs were blown in a large illuminated sign over the Showbar entrance announcing Welcome to Weston-super-Mare, and the rear of the building and neighbouring pool was a picture of sheer dilapidation.

But the town had not heard the last of Kingfisher, or at least its area manager Chris Sanderson. Undeterred by the problems his company had faced, in January 1991 he put forward a £2.8 million plan in similar vein but with important changes. Trading as Knightstone Leisure Ltd he proposed a complete upper floor in the Showbar for a ballroom and night-club and a ground-floor amusement arcade with Quasar, the latest American laser war game, as crowd-pulling centrepiece. The baths would be trans-formed with chutes and slides, but the conservatory for the yacht club site that had bedevilled the previous scheme was abandoned, as were the covered walkways. The bath-house was to become a theme pub and restau-rant and the Harbour Inn would open all day onto a Marine Lake alive with ice cream parlours, sun loungers, pedalos and canoes. Reassuringly he was reported as saying he had secured the necessary funding.

The official comment was that this scheme would be considered along-side any other the council might receive if it re-marketed the peninsula. But councillors, anxious to make progress, rejected that cautious approach of their officers and authorised talks with Mr Sanderson, which led to his winning an immediate concession to run the Harbour Inn and Marine Lake activities, followed by a 125-year lease. For normally sluggish local govern-ment it happened at unusual speed and despite other expressions of interest. One was from Philip Stubbs, owner of Birnbeck Pier, who pictured a Victo-rian-themed Knightstone with old-time music hall or cabaret nightclub.

The council explained that only Mr Sanderson could have opened the peninsula facilities that year as he had bought certain fixed items from Kingfisher. However, his plan was soon in trouble, and again the problem was licensing. Magistrates revoked the Showbar's 2am licence because of its under-use, jeopardising the chance of a nightclub. Without nightclub approval Mr Sanderson could not draw down investment funds, but he pressed on, hopeful of the necessary consent for an opening at Easter 1992.

Sunday dances were still being held at the Showbar while their usual Winter Gardens home was being renovated. On March 21, 1991 the Winter Gardens re-opened and the former Knightstone Theatre was never used again. Dance sessions did not transfer immediately because of resistance to the Winter Gardens' higher charges, and the exact date of their move is, regrettably, not recorded. But the curtain was finally falling on the 89-year-old venue of some of Weston's most vibrant and memorable entertainment, although no one knew that at the time.

Mr Sanderson's hopes were cruelly dashed when he excitedly rang Woodspring to announce the completion of architect plans to convert the baths to a fun pool, on which he had already spent £50,000. He was told the baths had just been grade-two listed which meant flues could not be routed through the roof as the design required. Special permission would be needed from the Environment Department, pushing back a likely start on conversion to March 1992. By the end of that year work had still not begun and now English Heritage was objecting to revised proposals for the baths as a ten-pin bowling centre.

Throughout 1993 it was the same story – the date kept slipping and the cost kept rising. By November Mr Sanderson's scheme had soared in price to £5 million but he confidently predicted a start later that month. The new official tourist brochure announced: 'Knightstone Island - Major New Complex Opening March 1994'. It was recklessly optimistic, for funding had not even been secured. Mr Sanderson diplomatically blamed the recession, equity investors' lack of confidence in leisure schemes generally and particular difficulties with Knightstone's listed buildings. From the safe distance of 20 years he can be more candid: 'I was chasing all over the country and abroad trying to raise £5 million and it was like bearing a cross. They all said "Oh no, not Weston, we don't like Weston". They thought Weston did nothing. Birnbeck Pier was falling to pieces, Knightstone was falling to pieces – there were all these problems and nothing was being done. And there was no support, I might add.'

It looked as if the project faced the same fate as Mr Stubbs' doomed marina at Birnbeck Pier and the council considered boarding up Knightstone's deteriorating buildings. Mr Sanderson missed deadline after deadline

The shabby state of the rear of the building after its permanent closure.

to raise the money and when one in March 1995 passed without progress he was allowed to continue running the Harbour Inn and Marine Lake for the summer but told to hand back the lease in October. In a triumph of hope over experience that limit was extended to January 1996 to give one last chance of securing finance. When the council itself was rebuffed in its bid for cash for Knightstone from Europe's Single Regeneration Budget Challenge Fund Mr Sanderson was the first to appreciate the irony.

A petition with several hundred names demanded no more lease extensions and that residents be given a chance to bid for the concessions and Knightstone Causeway parking that Mr Sanderson controlled as tenant. But in February 1996 it was announced he was selling his lease to Bristol-based BS Group, having little to show for his long and vexed involvement. The BS Group, an altogether more substantial concern which owned Bristol Rovers' former stadium, nightclubs and health clubs, promised a 'comprehensive leisure development' within existing consents and a grand opening for the 1997 summer. The new North Somerset Council, which replaced Woodspring, hoped for a high-quality scheme.

The forlorn-looking auditorium ended up being used to store Marine Lake pedalos.

As was often the case with Knightstone, the target date was wide of the mark and it was not until late 1997 that a planning application revealed the company had in mind a dance floor and ten-pin bowling at the former theatre, a nightclub having been ruled out after market research. Urgent action was needed as the Harbour Inn was still open in an area of appalling disrepair. The company focused efforts on converting the bath-house to a restaurant while the theatre building was used to store empty beer barrels, walkways becoming strewn with smashed crates and broken glass.

Just cleaning the bath-house stonework exposed all manner of problems that added £300,000 to the bill before they began. The building had sunk by four inches on one side and many areas were blighted by dry rot. Little of the original inside could be saved and section by section had to be removed and copied to comply with listed building conditions. An admirable restoration was completed but not until 2000, and while the Harbour Inn was also refurbished as a sports bar with ten televisions, the Showbar and baths remained untouched, and who knew what condition they were in underneath.

Councillors branded it a disaster area and called for their listed status to be removed so they could be demolished – a view backed in a poll conducted by the *Mercury*. Even as readers voted, clumps of masonry fell off in high winds and rain and at this rate they would end up with a listed pile of rubble, one councillor mordantly observed. In fact, although the baths had been listed in 1991, the Showbar was unlisted. However, all the talk of demolition rapidly saw it grade-two listed, which meant 'every effort' had to be made to preserve it but without any public funds to do so. It was an impossible situation: the building was uneconomic to run but couldn't be knocked down, and all the time the weather was tearing it apart.

The president of the Hotels' and Restaurants' Association complained that the area's unsightly builders' skips and rubbish were hitting tourism. Other businesses had prospered in the previous decade but generally ones like his had slumped in value by a quarter. As he spoke, the owners of The Rozel, a 40-bedroom hotel overlooking the site, announced they were closing as there was no longer any entertainment on offer for guests at their end of town. The *Mercury* doubted whether any other local authority would have so casually presided over the crumbling of such prominent buildings as those on the peninsula.

Correspondents hankered after Weston's enterprising past and lamented its new reputation for charity shops and drink and drug treatment centres. A nonagenarian wistfully recalled the vision and courage, now sadly lacking, of those who had built the promenade and beach lawns all those years ago. Where had the town's confidence gone? The Knightstone heyday generation mourned the Weston they once knew, with its art deco bus station, a victim of de-regulation, The Pool and its iconic diving stage and Rozel bandstand, never mind the fabulous shows and pantomimes. They dreaded the likely impact on roads and public services of proposed large housing developments and thought it unlikely they would retire to Weston today. Veteran councillor Ken Lacey, who had lived in the town all his life, viewed Knightstone, Birnbeck Pier and the Tropicana, which had closed in

Conversion to apartments under way in January 2007.

2000, as monuments to irresponsible local government over many years. Sooner or later, he said, someone would have to grasp the nettle.

The first to do so were former mayor John Crockford-Hawley and Dr Howard Smith, a local campaigner, who suggested converting the Showbar and baths to flats. In 2001 North Somerset Council demanded action. With days to go to a deadline it had imposed, BS Group announced that the two properties would be converted for residential use behind their preserved façades. At last a solution had been found to end years of decay.

There were complaints that a potential attraction was being lost. The Civic Society saw it as 'a symbolic failure to meet the challenge of the site' and predicted the end of Weston as a credible resort. Such a pessimistic outlook was countered by an initiative called Blue Skies, which called for a concerted effort to revive the tourist industry by exploiting new markets. Perhaps that was as much as the council and its predecessors could ever have done given their limited powers and tight budgets.

Six housing developers showed interest and by the end of 2001 Gaming

International, as BS Group had become, announced it had selected Redrow Homes. A long public consultation began and in May 2003 the Harbour Inn was closed and its six staff made redundant. Months went by without sight of a planning application and the fear was that designing a profitable scheme was proving challenging even for the expert conservation architects recruited. Eventually, financial questions blocking progress were resolved and it was reported that Redrow would buy up Gaming International's interests to become sole developer and leaseholder, splitting profits with the council.

Although Knightstone's future seemed settled, one last bid to revive the theatre was launched by John Redgrave, who cherished boyhood memories of working backstage in the 1950s. He planned to re-open it for cabaret, plays, films, exhibitions and conferences and felt sure hoteliers would welcome his attempt to restore the feel of a traditional holiday resort. He considered it 'the greatest tragedy' for the town that it had closed. 'It had a marvellous position, right on the sea-front, and was also the largest theatre in town. Weston needs Knightstone far more than it needs the Playhouse.' But nothing more was heard of his proposal after residential planning approval was granted.

Redrow's £25 million development comprised 87 one, two and three-bedroom flats in the former theatre, baths and bath-house and two new blocks called Knightstone Beacon and Pruen House. The theatre itself was converted to 26 flats and a café, but most of the ground floor, scene of nine decades of live entertainment, became nothing more glamorous than an internal car park. A café in the bath-house was named Dr Fox's Tearoom after the building's nineteenth-century founder. The first apartments, priced at £150,000 to £410,000, were completed by 2007 when the Queen and Prince Philip officially opened the complex – the only royal visit the theatre ever had, long after its doors had closed.

Today its preserved exterior is a lasting reminder to thousands of residents and holidaymakers of the vibrant shows enjoyed all those years ago. Residents such as Jean Jenkins who as a young child was taken by an 'aunt' to pantomimes in the 1930s, a Boxing Day treat for so many excited youngsters. 'We used to go quite a lot and sit in the cheaper seats at the back. It was a popular place and the standard of show was good. I was very sorry when it closed and would like it to have gone on as it was.'

Karan Simmons, a 14-year-old Mavdor dancer in *Aladdin* in 1961 who blossomed as Cinderella three years later, said: 'I'll never forget Knightstone

Developers preserved the theatre's exterior when converting it to residential use. New flats were added on the right.

in the winter – everyone had colds but it was a lovely time. Bob and Alf Pearson were sweet and kind and the stagehands were excellent. It breaks my heart to go past it now. You look over the ramparts and think, that was my dressing-room. It's really sad.'

Weston Dramatic Society veteran Ray Edbrooke summed up: 'It was an old theatre with very few conveniences for the public as well as the players. There was no Tannoy – a callboy got you on stage at the right time. The lavatory facilities were inadequate and the lights in the dressing-rooms were inadequate – it was that sort of place, but it had a great atmosphere. The key thing about these places is they've gone and won't return. It's to be regretted, but you can't bring the time back.'

During the conversion to flats, concrete poured into the basement staffroom to stabilise the building gradually submerged an immovable photo-gallery of stars who had graced the stage. Pearl Carr and Teddy Johnson's detachable picture found refuge at the Playhouse, but the fate of the others was a metaphor for the disappearance of a glorious entertainment era that would never be seen again.

Appendix

Knightstone Pavilion/Theatre shows
Edited to 1968; unedited thereafter

1902
May 13: Opening Night Concert, with Edith Grey-Burnand, May Coleman
May: Blue Viennese Band
June: HM Scots Guards' Band
National Association of Master Bakers and Confectioners Annual Conference lunch
July: Edison's Animated Pictures
November: Weston-super-Mare Chrysanthemum Society 17th Exhibition
December: Sherlock Holmes, with Ben Greet Company

1903
January: Wanderings in the Pacific, illustrated lecture by Dr Roxburgh
April: Thomas A Edison's Electric Animated Excursions: King's Coronation, Delhi Durbar
May: Weston-super-Mare Philharmonic Society Concert: Hiawatha, with Edith Evans, Charles Saunders, Montague Warlock, Edward Cook
June: Adeler and Sutton's Pierrots
July: Welsh Ladies' Choir
August: Florodora, with Ben Greet Company
Il Trovatore, with Neilson Grand Opera Company

1904
January: Clara Butt, Kennerley Rumford
February: FR Benson Shakespearean Company (North)
April: African Boys' Choir
May: Weston-super-Mare Philharmonic Society Grand Opera Night: The Bohemian Girl, with Adelaide Mullen, Henry Beaumont, Ottley Cranston, Eveline Gerrish, FE Shellabear, Edward Cook, W Darby, Frank Gardner's Orchestra
June: Our Navy (film)
August: Poole's Myriorama
October: Russo-Japanese War, illustrated lecture by Walter Kirton
November: Madame Albani

1905
January: A Trip Round the World, A Drama in the Air, Scenes of Japan Naval Life (films)
Before Port Arthur, illustrated lecture by Frederic Villiers
March: Gospel Services, with National Free Church Missioner Gipsy Smith
August: The Toreador, with Charles Fagan, Charles M Heslop, Grosvenor Orchestra
December: Aladdin, with Beatrice Varley, Louie Rodney

1906
February: Aladdin, with Iris Dimoline, Marjorie Dimoline, Sydal Roberts, Victor Dimoline, Percy Holway, in aid of St Paul's Church Building Fund
May: Church Defence Meeting on Education Bill, with Bishop of Bath and Wells Dr George Kennion, Lord Hylton

June: Life in Our Navy and Our Army (film)
July: Artificial Floral Exhibition and Sale, in aid of Crippled Girls' Industrial Branch
November: Mark Hambourg

1907
April: Naval and Military Display and Concert, with local companies of Royal Naval Volunteer Reserve, Royal Engineers Volunteers, Army Gymnastic Staff
August: Robin Hood; The Adventure of Lady Ursula, with Norman V Norman, Beatrice Wilson
October: Black Dike Band
Spiders - their Work and their Wisdom, with Rev Dr Dallinger
November: Fabbro's Electric Singing Pictures: Royal Review of Aldershot, The Derby 1907 (films)

1908
February: General Trades, Foods, Cycle and Industrial Exhibition
Looking for Trouble, illustrated lecture by Edgar Wallace
Red Riding Hood, with Dimo-Panto Company - Kathleen Webber, Percy Holway, Victor Dimoline, Sydal Roberts, Cecil Walker, Wilfred Roe, May Perrett, Iris Dimoline, Eunice Dimoline, Tillie Weir, Shamrock Orchestra, in aid of St Paul's Church Fund
April: The Mikado, with Wells Operatic Society - Fred Russ, Winifred Thomas, Henri Drayton, Harry Partridge, John Bishop, Ada Bennett, Robert Norton, H Gonzague Riviere
August: The Dairymaids, with Isa Bowman, Sam Lysons, Edwin Dobbs
September: Miss Hook of Holland, with Amy Grey

1909
January: Hospital Town Ball, with Royal Marine Light Infantry (Plymouth Division) Band
Primrose League Children's Dances, with Nora Gough's pupils; What Free Trade Did for Bill, with Weston Pierrots
National Union of Conservative Associations Somerset Division Meeting, with Sir Alexander Acland Hood
April: The Pirates of Penzance, with Weston-super-Mare Amateur Operatic Society - Leslie J Fursland, Winifred Thomas, R Hoare Byers, Ada Bennett, A Bingham Hall, RH Ward, John Moore, Miss P Tuckey, Mrs TW Roe, Mrs JH Stephenson, J Rushworth, in aid of Weston-super-Mare Hospital
June: Wedding ball for Henry Butt's daughter
August: The Merry Widow, with George Edwardes' Company
October: Budget Protest League Mass Meeting, with Sir Robert Finlay, Captain Sandys, RB Graves-Knyfton
November: Boswell's Royal Circus

1910
January: Trades and Inventions Exhibition, with 'Prince Ishmael'
April: The Gondoliers, with Weston-super-Mare Operatic Society - Winifred Thomas, R Hoare Byers, A Bingham Hall, Dorothy Tucker, Leslie J Fursland, Ralph H Ward, Mrs Treliving, Edith Lidstone, John Moore, in aid of Weston Hospital and St Paul's Building Fund
July: Herr Julian Kandt and his Austrian Blue Band
October: Scotties' Variety Combine, with Scott Alexander
The Importance of Being Earnest, with Mr and Mrs WA Gouldsmith, FC Ferguson, Mrs JM de Vine, Mr and Mrs Tom Pethick, Evelyn Gordon, in aid of Weston Hospital and Royal National Hospital for Consumption and Diseases of the Chest, Ventnor
English Opera Singers: Frederic Dale, Edith Serpell, Gertrude Macaulay, Dora Beedlestone, Harold Loprest
December: Mass Meeting of Liberal Men, with CE Hobhouse MP, Lord Haversham

1911

January: Penn-Strangways Company Character Sketches and Songs, in aid of Weston-super-Mare Primrose League
February: Electric Moving Pictures: Fabian Smokes Strong Tobacco, Her Dolly in Danger, Rome, its Monuments and Cascades, The Evening Story, Wiffles Goes Fishing, Picturesque Scenes in the Loffoden Islands, The New Butler, Lorenzo, The Captain's Bride, Dances in Silhouette
March: Bioscope Lecture: Miss Weston's Work in the Royal Navy
May: A Night in the House of Commons, lecture by William 'Mabon' Abraham MP
July: Shakespeare plays, with Alexander Marsh, Carrie Baillie
November: Hancock's Trust: Recent Knowledge of the Starry Heavens, illustrated lecture by Royal Observatory Chief Assistant AS Eddington

1912

February: Dimo-Panto Company: Dick Whittington
Wells Division Liberal Association Public Meeting, with John Muldoon MP, John Schnuck, CT Grinfield and orchestra
April: British Empire Shakespeare Society Weston branch Shakespeare Birthday Celebration: The Merry Wives of Windsor, with FW Bere, WG Harrison, E Avern, AE Catford, Mrs Needham, Mrs Treliving, TW Williams, in aid of RMS Titanic Mansion House Fund
July: Chinston Wurchill's Experiments (film)
November: Hancock's Trust: Whales and Whale Fishing, lantern lecture by Frank T Bullen

1913

January: A Christmas Fairy Play: The Cricket on the Hearth, with Dimo-Panto Company and Adelphians
March: FR Benson Shakespearean Company (South)
April: Kinemacolor: With our King and Queen through India (film)

1914

February: The Witch o' Worlebury, with Adelphians, Katharine Blott's pupils, AG Dowding, Weston Amateur Orchestra, in aid of Whitecross Hall Fund and St John Ambulance Store
March: Marie Hall
July: Banquet for French and Belgian journalists, with Mogg's Military Prize Band
November: Weston Recruiting Evening, with Paymaster-General Lord Strachie

1915

February: Egypt - Our New Protectorate, illustrated lecture by Canon WR Yates, in aid of Ashcombe House Hospital
August: Grumpy, with Robertson Hare
October: The German Spy Peril, lecture by William Le Queux
The War! Why has God Permitted it? When and How will it End?, lecture by Gospel Forward Movement

1916

February: Military Concert, with 3/4 Royal Berkshire Regiment, Katharine Blott's pupils
Clara Butt, John Booth, in aid of Clara Butt-Rumford Fund
April: Raffles, the Amateur Cracksman
September: Shakespearean Tercentenary Festival, with Florence Glossop-Harris, Henry Baynton
October: Concert, with blind musicians, in aid of St Dunstan's Hostel for Blinded Soldiers and Sailors

Pavilion closed for war use

1917
June: At the Front with the YMCA, lecture by Cameron Highlanders' Padre Rev John McNeil
July: English Opera Company
November: War Savings Patriotic Meeting, with National Committee's Major Rigg, Mogg's Military Prize Band

1918
February: Mass Meeting, with Dock, Wharf, Riverside and General Workers' Union general secretary Ben Tillett MP
April: Weston Amateur Minstrels, Leslie Fursland, Wallace Taylor, Ralph Ratcliffe, Rev JHH Doorbar, in aid of Weston-super-Mare General Hospital and VPC (Vegetable Products Committee) Fund for the Sailors in the North Sea
The Private Secretary, with Weston-super-Mare Amateur Dramatic Society - HH Brightwell, Martin Brown, Mrs C Tolley, Dr JG Cooper, Grace Nancarrow, Marjorie Dimoline, AG Dowding, Mr Jennings' Band, in aid of Weston-super-Mare General Hospital
October: British and Foreign Sailors' Society Trafalgar Day Sailors' Demonstration and Centenary Celebration, with Vice-Admiral AP Stoddart, Winifred Hamilton, Weston-super-Mare Amateur Orchestra, in aid of Lady Jellicoe's Fund
November 14: Thanksgiving Service, with Rector the Rev Prebendary B Norton Thompson, Rev John Holden, Rev William Chadwick, Rev HH Turner, Henry Ward

1919
March: League of Nations Public Meeting, with J Hugh Edwards MP, Prebendary B Norton Thompson
May: Great Naval Night Concert, with Marmaduke Alford, May Witchell, Seymour Dossor, Wallace A Taylor, Marian Hillman, Rear-Admiral C Winnington-Ingram
December: Adventures in the Antarctic, illustrated lecture by Sir Ernest Shackleton

1920
January: Primrose League Fancy Dress Ball, with Mr Ebb's Orchestra
How We Keep the Seas, illustrated lecture by Captain Teddy Evans
May: Missionary Exhibition: Africa and the East, with the Bishops of Bath and Wells and Taunton
June: Flannel and Muslin Ball, in aid of Weston-super-Mare Creche

1921
March: An Actor's View of Shakespeare, with Sir Johnston Forbes-Robertson
May: The Admirable Crichton (film)
July: Pygmalion, with Charles Macdona's Company

1922
March: Weston-super-Mare Orpheus Glee Society 16th Annual Concert, with Madame Kirkby Lunn, Edward Cook
December: The Sleeping Beauty, with Carlton Fredrick's Company

1923
January: RA Maddox's Cinderella
March: Weston-super-Mare Incorporation public meeting
April: Sir Frank Benson, Genevieve Townsend
October: Rob Roy (film)
December: Weston-super-Mare Liberal Eve-of-Poll Rally

1924
February: M Moiseiwitsch recital
Wessex RE, British Legion and 4th Somerset Light Infantry Military Ball, with Royal Engineers' String
Band, Chatham, in aid of British Legion

1925
February: Hospital Extension Fund public meeting, with hospital president Henry Butt, council chairman
Ernest Stradling
March: Zeebrugge (film)
April: Herman Darewski and his Band

1926
June: National Liberal Federation Council Annual Conference, with David Lloyd George, Viscount Grey
of Fallodon, Sir Donald Maclean, Sir John Simon, Frank Murrell
October: Cherry Kearton and chimpanzee Mary; With Cherry Kearton in the Jungle (film)

1927
September: Wilkie Bard
Lilian Burgess, JH Scotland
December: Cinderella, with Jack Foster, Joan Fuller

1928
March: United Commercial Travellers' Association Grand Charity Dance, with Blackmore Vale Band
October: HMV Record Recital
November: Verdun (film)
December: Handel's Messiah, with Weston-super-Mare Choral Society

1929
January: Peter Pan (film)
July: The Passing of the Third Floor Back, The Waiting Game, with Frank Forbes-Robertson, Miss
Sydney Thornton
August: National Orchestra of Wales Concert, with Warwick Braithwaite, Heddle Nash
December-January: Jack and Jill, with Dorothy Tavenor, Doreen Earnshaw, Muriel Millington, Low
Charlesworth

1930
January: Carnival Ball, with Alf Read and his Paragon Players, in aid of Somerset Flooded Areas Distress
Fund
February: The Silver Box, with Red Triangle Players
March: Travelogue: Canada: The Spirit of a Great Dominion, with Alfred Ward, TE Macfarlane
April: Weston-super-Mare Orpheus Glee Society Fourth Annual Concert, with Rebe Hillier, Leonard
Dennis, Edward Cook, Marion Hillman, Frank Shellabear
Boxing Tournament, with Mogg's Military Prize Band
May: GWR Social and Educational Union Annual Conference music festival
Ye Elizabethan Fayre and Maske, with Weston-super-Mare Operatic and Dramatic Societies, in aid of
Jubilee Appeal for Church of England Waifs and Strays Society
December-January: Sinbad the Sailor, with Olivette Haydon, Nora Roden, Frank Jewks, Harry Stafford

1931
March: Jan Kubelik
Grand Concert, with Mary Cadbury, William Parsons, Evelyn Revalde, Hedley Goodall, HC Burgess,

Ladies' GOK Choir, Dorothy Palmer, Seymour Dossor, Mary Dossor, in aid of Choral Society and Mid-Somerset Musical Competitions Festival
August: Ronald Frankau and party
Alexander and Mose (Billy Bennett and Albert Whelan)
November: OO-Tang (film)
December-January: Humpty Dumpty, with Fred Brady, Jack Land, Sylvia Johns, Olivette Haydon

1932
March: St Patrick Day's Ball, with Bath Pump Room Dance Band, in aid of Warehousemen, Clerks and Drapers' Schools
May: National Association of Local Government Officers' Conference, with Minister of Mines Isaac Foot
July: Wee Georgie Wood, Coram and 'Jerry', Adele Verne, Lucille Benstead
August: Mona Grey and Party
Debroy Somers and his Band
Alexander and Mose (Billy Bennett and Albert Whelan)
September: Teddy Brown
October: Shakespeare plays, with Allan Wilkie, Miss Hunter-Watts, Alexander Marsh
Round Africa with Cobham (film)
November: HMV Gramophone Recital
British Legion Boxing Tournament, in aid of Somerset County Legion funds
December: Somerset Christmas Market, with Alf Read and his Paragon Players
December: Cinderella, with Gwen Crystal, Constance Lake, Freddie Fay

1933
April: Elsie and Doris Waters
Peg o' My Heart, with Gerald Alexander Repertory Company
May: Wembley Empire Colossal Circus
June: The Beggar's Opera
July: The Girl from Woolworths, with Joan Coleridge, June Radbourne and the June Dancers, Reginald Andrews, Billy Rowland
August: Gwen Farrar and Party
Anton Dolin and Party
September: Magic Mania, with The Great Carmo, Sybil Elsie
November: Climbing Mount Everest, lecture by CG Crawford
Eugène Ltd presents Waves of Desire hair fashion revue, with Ivy Tresmand
December: Jack and the Beanstalk, with Irene Rose, Freddy Fitts, Beatrice Ewens

1934
January: Grand New Year Ball, with Regalians Dance Band, in aid of Royal Merchant Seamen's Orphanage
Babes in the Wood, with Mildred Redfern, Phyllis Weeks, Marjorie James, Ruth Brandon, Jean Pratt, Violet Mullery, Keith Tyler, Victor Dimoline, Wilfred Roe, FB Hollis, Spencer Bartlett, Leslie Titley, Roy Vickery, Charles Cole, George Bosley, Zillah Worth, Frank Gee, in aid of British Legion National Conference Hospitality Fund
April: Paul Robeson
The Flitch Trial, with Sir Duncan Grey, Leslie Fursland, in aid of Weston-super-Mare Hospital and commercial traveller charities
August: The Scarlet Empress (film)
October-November: Monsieur Beaucaire, with Weston-super-Mare Dramatic Society - Keith Tyler, Blueflower Betts, Warren Powell, Esme Britton, Walter H Brown, Gordon Reid, in aid of District Nursing Association and Weston Hospital

December: Babes in the Wood, with Dora and Vera Compton, Montague Biggs, Wilfred Brandon

1935
January: Alice in Wonderland (film)
Weston-super-Mare British Legion pantomime Robinson Crusoe, with Esme Dunning-Moore, Phyllis Weeks, Wilfred Roe, Keith Tyler, Roy Vickery, Kitty Mogg, Victor Dimoline, Frank Hollis, HE Dymond, Leslie Titley, Freda Vickery, Mildred Vickery, Jean Pratt, W Blewitt, George Bosley, Zillah Worth, Mavdor Troupe
February: High Class and Speed Variety with principals from Bristol's Prince's Theatre pantomime
William Joyce, British Union of Fascists Director of Propaganda
July: Sir Oswald Mosley, British Union of Fascists leader
November: Palestine Exhibition, opened by Bishop of Bath and Wells, in aid of Church Mission to Jews
Modern Homes Exhibition
December: Dick Whittington and his Cat, with WH Lester, George Fairweather, Gerald Farrar and his Rhythm Boys

1936
May: Mary, Mary, Quite Contrary, with HA Charman
June: Out of the Blue, with Ronnie Brandon, Dickie Pounds, Eddie Reinhart
Urban District Councils of England and Wales Conference
July-September: The Show of Shows, with Mona Vivian, Peter Paget, Gordon Freeman, Peggy Ford-Carrington, Will Hay Junior, Joan Hay
August: Billy Cotton and his Band
Teddy Joyce and his Band
Albert Sandler and Trio, Sybil Roe
Charlie Kunz
September: Nat Gonella and his Georgians, Peggy Ford-Carrington
The Phantom Five
Harry Pell's Premiers
October: Opening of the Season Ball, with Reginald Williams and his Futurists Bristol Coliseum Band, in aid of Weston Rugby Club
Church Mission Society lectures, in aid of CMS Hospital, Quetta, India
November: The Ghost Train, with Weston-super-Mare Dramatic Society - Victor Dimoline, Walter H Brown, Ruth Dening, John Westwood, Mark Tyler, Janet Brown, Warren Powell, Eileen Marshall, Paul Dening, Keith Tyler, Leighton Norman, Jack Watson, Francis Nugent, Lester Lane
December: Le Gendre de Monsieur Poirier; Fables de la Fontaine, with Les Comediens de Paris
Red Riding Hood, with Tom Dixon, Frances Kinders, Edna Green

1937
July-September: The Show of Shows, with Billy Bernhart, Marion Dawson, Peggy Ford-Carrington
August: George Robey
September: Charter Celebration Concert, with Al Lever and Charter Ball Orchestra
The Summer Revellers, with David Graves, Gwen Adeler, Patricia Gallagher, Sydney Barnes
October: Guy Fawkes Carnival Miss Somerset Ball, with Al Lever and Special Syncopated Dance Band
Barnardo Musical Boys
November: Exhibition billiards and snooker, with Joe Davis
Full House, with Weston-super-Mare Dramatic Society - Constance Chapman, Keith Tyler, Paul Dening, Mildred Norman, Leighton Norman, Esme Painter, Victor Dimoline
December: Cinderella, with Billy Wooley, Bessie Evans, Edyth King

1938

February: Ali Baba and the Forty Thieves, with Charles Dorning, Greta Cousins, Don Charsley, Ronnie Austin, Gladys Brittain, Hilda Leyden, Marie Gilbert, Nora Frampton, Edna Bradley
Weston-super-Mare Conservative and Unionist Association meeting, with Postmaster General Major GC Tryon, Lord Bayford, Weston-super-Mare MP Ian Orr Ewing
Somerset Constabulary County Ball, with 12th Royal Lancers' Dance Orchestra
April: Dances and Ballets, with Katharine Blott's pupils; Columbine to Wed, with Mrs Cuthbert Hicks' pupils, in aid of Weston-super-Mare General Hospital
July-September: Out of the Hat, with Eddie Reinhart, Ernest Bertram, Foulger and Electra, Charles Grossman and his Symphonic Septette
September: Weston's Own Variety, with Ivor Moreton and Dave Kaye, Ronald Gourley, Waldini and his Gypsy Band
October: Benefit Concert for HC Burgess, with Charles Dorning and the Municipal Orchestra, Bratza, Lance Dossor, Hooper Bussell, Doris Mogridge, Robert Cole, Noelle Watson, Leonard Rice
Regency Revels and Fayre, with Alexander School of Dancing, Winthorpe Academy of Dancing, Red Triangle Orchestra, in aid of Church of England Waifs and Strays Society
November: Snooker and Billiards, with Joe Davis
December: Christmas Dream and Fantasy

1939

March: A Flitch Trial, with Leslie Fursland, in aid of Weston Hospital and commercial traveller charities
The Mikado, with Weston-super-Mare Operatic Society - Walter H Brown, Frank Lane, Leslie Fursland, Lewis Stuckey, Joyce Tidman, Lem Kinsey, in aid of Weston-super-Mare Hospital
April: Co-operative Party Conference, with Clement Attlee MP
Crazy Days, with Barry Lupino, Gretchen Franklin, Wyn Weaver, Billy Mayerl
April-August: Weston Repertory Company: George and Margaret, Black Limelight, The Late Christopher Bean, I Killed the Count, Yes and No, It's a Boy, Housemaster, A Cuckoo in the Nest, Pygmalion, Dear Brutus, The Wind and the Rain, The Amazing Dr Clitterhouse, Fresh Fields, The Scarlet Pimpernel, Hay Fever
August: Billy Bennett, Stanley Holloway, Tiller Girls
Renee Houston and Donald Stewart, Sydney Phasey and his Broadcasting Orchestra
Evelyn Laye, Gordon Whelan, Bennett and Williams
Billy Scott-Coomber and his Singing Grenadiers, Suzette Tarri
Carroll Levis and his BBC Discoveries, Cyril Levis, Tessie O'Shea
Claude Dampier, Billie Carlyle, The Two Leslies

Theatre closed for a week on declaration of war

September-December: Weston Repertory Company: Tony Draws a Horse, French Without Tears, Too Young to Marry, French Leave, The Importance of Being Earnest, The Shining Hour, The Middle Watch, While Parents Sleep, Saint Joan, Grouse in June, All the King's Horses, The Greeks had a Word for It
December-January: Alf's Button of 1940, with Harry Emeric, Fred Culpitt, Richard Neller, Clarice Clare, Sydney Barnes, Constance Chapman, Andrews Buck, Keith Dimoline

1940

January-July: Weston Repertory Company: Robert's Wife, Quiet Wedding, The Bat, Without the Prince, The Chinese Bungalow, Goodness, How Sad, Love from a Stranger, Fair and Warmer, Dangerous Corner, As you Are, For the Love of Mike, Should the Doctor Tell?, Gas Light, Peg O' My Heart, Full House, Night Must Fall, Bird in Hand, Dear Octopus, White Cargo, Three for Luck, Yellow Sands, Saloon Bar, Room for Two
June: Pierre Daninos, Royal Engineers French liaison officer

September: Nazi War Machine, lecture by Bernard Newman

Theatre closed for war use

1942
April: Randolph Sutton, Leslie James, Iris Sadler, Cilla's Football Dogs
July: Inter-Allied Variety Week, with Captain Strelsky and his Russian Cossack Band and Choir, Helen Binnie
Big Bill Campbell's Rocky Mountain Rhythm
August: Hello, America, with Nor Kiddie, Wilson, Keppel and Betty
Lady, Meet the Navy, with Leslie Fuller, Frank Formby, Tommy Dee, Bebe Helene
Rawicz and Landauer, Howard Rogers, Bob Bemand and his Pigeons
September: Rookery Nook, with Benson Repertory Company
December: Dick Whittington and his Cat, with Benson Repertory Company, Mavdor Girls

1943
February: Red Army Day: 25th Anniversary Celebration, in aid of Mrs Churchill's Aid to Russia Fund
April: Love in the Mist, with Donald Pleasence, Christine Bennett, Miriam Raymond
Ladies Out of Uniform, with Joe King, Patricia Stainer, Charles Jones and Vic Thomas, Joan and Jean Franklin, Cleff and Moroney
Me and My Girl, with Barry Lupino, Helen Barnes, Fred A Leslie, Molly Stoll
May: Elsie and Doris Waters, Kemble Kean and Laurel Mather, Lucille, Charles Ancaster
The Squire's Party, with Morris and Cowley, Johnson Clark, Percy Pryde
Herman Darewski and his Radio Band, Mona Grey
Ride 'em Cowboy, with Buck Warren and Chic, Pat O'Brien, Larry Jay
June: Josie Fearon and Charles Gillespie, Tom Gamble, Melville Birley, Herschel Henlere
Issy Bonn
Harry Benet's International Circus
Kenneth and George Western, Terina, Geddes Brothers, Russ Carr
It's All Yours, with Cyril Dowler, Kathleen West, Dot and Dash
July: Top-Notchers, with Maurice Colleano
August: A Date in Tunis, with Leslie Fuller, Maisie Weldon
Sandy Powell, Eve Drury
The Chocolate Soldier, with Sydney Burchall, Kitty Reidy, Darroll Richards
October: Ballet Rambert

1944
June: A Hundred Children Calling, with Greta Cousins' pupils
August: Zuider Zee, with Macari and his Dutch Accordion Serenaders
Florodora, with Jay Laurier, Kittie Prince
September: Roy Lester, Steffani and his Silver Songsters, Ronalde, Jack Cranston
Ballets Jooss
November: Boxing Tournament, in aid of St Dunstan's and National Institute for the Blind
December: 8th (Weston) Battalion, Somerset Home Guard, Stand Down Parade
Babes in the Wood, with Mignon Jarrold, Mavdor Babes

1945
May: Twinkle, with Clarkson Rose, Olive Fox, Eddie Childs
Weston-super-Mare and District Civil Defence Unit, Somerset No 3 Area, Stand Down Celebration
July: Stars of Radio, with Judy Shirley and Sam Browne
Radio Funfare, with The Two Leslies, Don Phillipe and Marta

Take it Easy, with Terry Cantor, Eddie Hart, Alec Duck
August: Douglas Byng, Dorothy Ward, Alan Kitson
September: 'Can I Do you Now, Sir?', with Dorothy Summers, Dino Galvani, Horace Percival, Sydney Keith, Billy Scott-Coomber
December: Dick Whittington and his Cat, with Mignon Jarrold, Theo Lambert, David Graves

1946
March: Jenny Villiers, with Bristol Old Vic Company - Pamela Brown, Faith Brook, William Devlin, Dan Cunningham, Yvonne Mitchell, Noel Williams, Nora Nicholson, Kenneth Connor, Gerald Welch, Anthony Hudson, Noel Willmass, John Garside, Peter Reynolds, Derrick Penly, Gerard McLarnon, Douglas Rye, Patrick Troughton, Colin Eaton, Karl Hass
June-September: Summer Rhapsody, with Frank O'Brian, Herschel Henlere, Forsythe, Seamon and Farrell, The Two Leslies, Robb Wilton, Suzette Tarri, Ronald Frankau and Monte Crick, Adelaide Hall, Hutch (Leslie A Hutchinson)
December: Aladdin, with Kay Lambert, Betty Pugh, David Graves, Leslie Rome, Vedras and Mack, Steve Daniels, George Sylvester, Sydney Barnes, Mavdor Girls, Mavdor Babes

1947
June-September: Summer Rhapsody, with Nan Kenway and Douglas Young, Tony Scott and Jimmy Duncan
September: Strike a New Note, with Freddie Frinton, Freddie Desmond and Jack Marks
For Laughing out Loud, with Maurice Colleano and family, Josie Fearon and Charles Gillespie, Elsie Bower
They're Off!, with Nita Valerie and Alice Day, Gray, Austin and Worth, Jackson Earle,
October: The Rose Without a Thorn, with Weston-super-Mare Dramatic Society - Leslie Titley, Anthea Crundall, Walter Brown, Leighton Norman, Adrian Gee, Vernon Webber, Leon Godby, Gertrude Stannard, Mary Wood, Alison Lundman, Victor Dimoline, Sydal Roberts
December: Mother Goose, with Theo Lambert, Dorothy Martell, Kay Lambert, Bertie Robbins, Sydney Barnes

1948
March: Out of the Blue, with David Graves, Norman Wisdom, Dickie Pounds, Ronnie Brandon, Patricia Cullen
June: Jane of the Daily Mirror, Eddie Reindeer
Hello from SEAC: Official 14th Army Revue
Would You Believe It!, with Pete Collins, Cleef and Moroney, Lofty, Pippi, Elroy, Crotchet, Engler's Educated Sheep
July: Morris and Cowley, Herschel Henlere, Jack Muldoon Four
Felix Mendelssohn and his Hawaiian Serenaders
Wilson, Keppel and Betty, Reg Dixon, Cynthia and Gladys, Peter Raynor
Suzette Tarri, Ravel, Sheikh Ben Ali
August: Billy Cotton and his Band, Alan Breeze
Jack Train, Three Hooper Sisters
Dutch Mill, with Macari and his Dutch Serenaders
Monte Rey, Bert Waller, Billy and Irene Kosmo, Boswell Twins, Ernest Arnley and Gloria
September: Hit Parade of 1948, with Paddy O'Neill, Carl and Roger Yale, Douglas Maynard, Tom Payne and Vera Hilliard, Ted and George Durante, Leslie Compton, Moira Day, Jean Sweetman
Battle of Britain Week Remembrance Concert, with Bryan Rodwell, Joy Newall, Eric Welch, RAF No 3 Regional Band
November: Shakespeareana-Internationale
December-February: Jack and the Beanstalk, with Babs Smart, David Graves, Suzanne Wild

1949
May: Magpie Masquerade, with Cyril Fletcher, Betty Astell, Harry Secombe
July: Max Miller, Helen Binnie, De Haven and Page
Hutch, Bert Shrimpton
August: Douglas Byng, Kay Cavendish, Hengler Brothers
Peter Cavanagh, Dorothy Ward, Alan Kitson
Eric Barker and Pearl Hackney, Jack Watson, Jack Mayer
Elsie and Doris Waters
Radio Forfeits, with Michael Miles, Patricia Rossborough, Ted and George Durante, Frank Preston,
Silvestri
September: Beryl Orde, Eddie Hardy, Walter Niblo
Max Wall, Nan Kenway and Douglas Young
December-February: Puss in Boots, with Bertie Robbins, Phyllis Terrell, Jackie Moggridge, David
Graves, Margaret Kent, Archie Wallen, Sydney Barnes

1950
July: Please Teacher, with Eddie Molloy, Diane Verne, Helen Ford, Norman Yeomans
Max Miller, Three Karloffs, Skating Dexters, Alfred Thripp
The Piddingtons, Semprini, Syd Plummer, 'Daisy May' and Saveen
Billy Cotton Band Show, with Doreen Stephens, Alan Breeze, Clem Bernard, Tattersall with 'Jerry'
Cavan O'Connor, Dorothy and David Lupino, Eddy Bayes, Les Cygne Four, Cycling Astons
August: Adelaide Hall, Harry Secombe
The George Mitchell Glee Club, with George Mitchell, Barbara Hope, James Armstrong, Alan Young
Five Smith Brothers, Wilson, Keppel and Betty, Eva May Wong, Frances Duncan, Joan Hinde
Stars of Radio, with Elsie and Doris Waters, Tony Walsh, Lorraine, Murray and Hinton, Ray and Madge
Lamar
September: Felix Mendelssohn and his Hawaiian Serenaders, Bert Shrimpton
Billy Reid and Dorothy Squires, Morecambe and Wise, Fred Lovelle, Bob Bemand's Comedy Pigeons
Binnie Hale, Bert Waller, Joe Church, Peter Dulay
The Squadronaires
December-February: Goody Two Shoes and the Yellow Dwarf, with Lucy Loupe, Phyllis Terrell, Theo
Lambert, Sydney Barnes

1951
July: Macari and his Dutch Serenaders
Richard Murdoch, Chevalier Brothers
Piccadilly Hayride, with Vic Gordon, Peter Colville, Sherman Fisher Girls, Hengler Brothers
August: Ella Shields, Douglas 'Cardew' Robinson, Bert Shrimpton
Randolph Sutton and Brian Seymour, Kitty Bluett, Edith Lewin, Algy More
Harry Lester and his Hayseeds
September: Sky High, with Reg Varney, Marriott and Wenman, Jacqueline Farrell, Peter Dulay
Suzette Tarri, La Celeste
Nat Mills and Bobbie
A Guardsman's Cup of Tea, with Rosalinde Fuller, Betty Huntley-Wright, Brian Nissen, David Airey,
John Nicholson
October: Jane Eyre, with Red Triangle Players - June Ellison, Leslie A Scamp, Margaret Couch, Joyce
Brooks, Toni Douglas, Denise Frampton
December-February: Queen of Hearts, with Sylvia Haskell, Irene Dickson, Sydney Barnes, George Ford,
Bernie Robbins, George Sylvester

1952

June: Vic Templar and Della Sweetman present Cinderella on Ice

Magpie Masquerade, with Cyril Fletcher, Cherry Lind, Gordon Holdom

July: Burton Lester's Midgets, Gloria's Dogs and Pigeons

Betty Driver, Alan Kitson

Arthur Lucan

August: Maudie Edwards

Sid Millward and his Nitwits

Frankie Howerd, Blanchie Moore, Robert Moreton and his Bumper Fun Book, Max Geldray, Marcia Owen

September: Music and Madness, with Fred Ferrari, Ken Morris, Len Marten, Vic Gordon and Peter Colville

This Was the Army, with Jack Lewis, Tommy Rose, Arthur Knotto, Dulay Brothers, Sonny Dawkes

Me and My Girl, with Lauri Lupino Lane, Wallace Lupino

Lilac Time, with Ronald Hill, Bertram Dench

November: Conservative Mass Meeting, with WF Deedes MP, Ian Orr Ewing MP for Weston-super-Mare

Merrie England, with Weston-super-Mare Operatic Society - Joyce Rainbow, Tom Thonger, Arthur Huxham, Bob Maguire, Bill Leonard, Margaret Minifie, Pearl Brookman, Rona Campbell, Rod McAulay, Ronny Benwell, Ted Lovell, Bill Clout, Fred Dove, Stanley Banwell, Leon Godby

December-February: Old King Cole, with Randolph Sutton, Sydney Barnes, Joy Pearse, June Fenton, Ron Rowlands, Wyn Calvin, Bertie Robins, Terry Doogan

1953

July: Piccadilly Hayride, with Terry Scott, Bill Maynard

Carroll Levis' BBC Discoveries, with Carroll Levis, Violet Pretty

Educating Archie, with Peter Brough and 'Archie Andrews', Mary Naylor, Ossie Noble

August: Joyce Golding, Malcolm Mitchell Trio, Dawn White and her Glamazons, Bobbie Kimber and 'Augustus Peabody'

Evening Stars, with Vic Gordon and Peter Colville, Wilson, Keppel and Betty, John Berryman

Elsie and Doris Waters, Aerial Kenways, Schichtl-Rulan's Marionettes and Robots

Gladys Morgan, Frank Laurie, Joan Laurie, Bert Hollman

September: Semprini, Bernard Miles, Paul and Peta Page, Walter Niblo

Double programme: Radio Fanfare, with Arthur Thripp, Vic Merry, Wally Brennan; Golden Prairie, with stars from Big Bill Campbell's Old Log Cabin

October: Continental Ballet, with Molly Lake, Travis Kemp, Monique Boam, Colin Worth

Tonight's the Night, with Somerset Police Entertainers, Constabulary Dance Orchestra

November: Jehovah's Witnesses Circuit Assembly

British Legion Festival of Remembrance, with Norman Brooks and his Broadcasting Orchestra

December-January: Mother Goose, with Mary Redfern, Terry Fearis, Al Rogers, Theo Hook, Sydney Barnes, Len Howe

1954

April: Greta Cousins presents A Hundred Children Calling, with Doris Philpott, in aid of the blind of Somerset

Hedley Claxton's Gaytime, with Ken Roberts, Rex Bashley, Rowena Vincent, Geoffrey Riley, Gladys Cowper

May: The Archers, with Ross Hutchinson, Marjorie Wilde, Desmond Tester, Gretchen Franklin, Michael Peake, Ann Johnson, Norman Johns

June: Out of the Blue, with Ronald Brandon, Joe York, Felix Bowness

The Fol-de-Rols, with Jack Tripp, Kathleen West, Leslie Crowther, Tudor Evans, Chris Carlsen

Masquerade, with Cyril Fletcher, Margaret Eves, Frankie Desmond, Gordon Holdom

July: Jimmy Young, Jack Martin, Joan Hinde, Dickie Henderson, Fred Atkins, Billy Baxter

Ronnie Ronalde, Arturo Steffani and orchestra, Darly's Dogs

Peter Brough and 'Archie Andrews', Ronald Chesney, Peter Madden, Ossie Noble

August: Elsie and Doris Waters, Edith Lewin, Dave King, Roy Stevens, Swan and Leigh
Harry Secombe, Sidney Burchall,
The Carroll Levis Television Show, with Carroll Levis, Violet Pretty, Barry Took, Dave Gray, Eddie
Wood
Ralph Reader's Once in a Laughtime, with Reg 'Confidentially' Dixon, Beryl Orde, Ted Carson, Norman
Fellows
September: Bob and Alf Pearson, Harry Paulo and Betty, Jean Roy, Johnson Clark
Hold your Breath, with Bob Andrews, Collins and Elizabeth, Al Carthy
Continental Ballet, with Molly Lake, Monique Boam, Richard Brown
November: National Children's Home Festival of Youth, with Sooty and Harry Corbett, Regency Girls'
Choir, Greta Cousins' dancers
December-January: Dick Whittington and his Cat, with Edith Lewin, Ann Redgrave, Wilson Harvey,
Sydney Barnes, Bobby Bent, Two Aberdonians

1955
April: Stars of Radio and Television, with Harold Berens, Ernest Arnley and Gloria, John Martin, Dennis
Spicer
Billy Graham Relays, by land line from Kelvin Hall, Glasgow - Weston-super-Mare Crusade
May: Hector Ross Radio Productions feature for Radio Luxembourg
June: Billie Anthony
July: Lester Ferguson
Lita Roza, Cardew Robinson, Nat Gonella
GH Elliott, Dawn White and her Glamazons
August: Ossie Morris, Tony Fayne and David Evans, Four Kelroys
Peter Cavanagh, Joyce Golding, Tony Stuart, Aerial Kenways
Max Wall, Joan Mann
Ray Ellington Quartet, Marion Ryan, Bud Ritchie
September: Dr Crock and his Crackpots
Robb Wilton, Sonny Jenks and Madeline Hearne, Vic Sanderson
Will Hammer presents Holiday Highlights, with Sonny Farrar, Fred Hugh, Joan Rudd, Robert Hargreaves
December: Festival of Queens, with Harry Corbett and Sooty, Winthorpe Academy pupils, in aid of
National Children's Home
December-January: Babes in the Wood, with Dan Sherry, Irene Bruce, Clare Delys, Alan Ridley, Harry
Pringle, Len Howe

1956
March: Sandy Powell and Kay White, Charles Stewart and Ann Matthews, Doreen Lane, Spense and
Davies, Les Murphy, Pamela Cundell, Mavdor Dancers
May: I am a Camera, with Keith Salberg Company
June: Masquerade, with Cyril Fletcher, Maureen Lane, Norman Caley, Gordon Holdom
Demonstration of Healing, with Harry Edwards of Temple of Divine Healing
Carroll Levis with his Revlon £1,000 Star Search, with Benson Dulay
Zip Goes a Million, with Tom Moss, Betty Jones, Gerry Barton, Valerie Wynn
July: Richard Murdoch, Edith Lewin, Joyce Golding and Tony Stuart, Jimmy Rogers and his Elusive Doves
August: Hedley Ward Trio, Ossie Morris
Tanner Sisters, Harold Berens, Bernard and Miss Radar, Pamela Cundell, Les Murphy
Elsie and Doris Waters, Walter Niblo, Marion Sanders, Kelroys, Eva May Wong, Mavdor Dancers
Gladys Morgan, Frank Laurie, Joan Laurie, Bert Hollman, Mary Genn and James O'Neill, Freddie
Harrison, Three Gridneffs, Skating Eiresons, Four Cassandras, Bert Shrimpton, Mavdor Dancers, Eric
Austin and Knightstone Orchestra
September: Four Jones Boys, Aerial Kenways, Ladringlos, Ford and Sheen, Pat and Howell Evans,

Marion Sanders, Sydney Shaw, Duo Russmar, Johnny Dallas, Mavdor Dancers
Thanks for the Memory, with GH Elliott, Hetty King, Randolph Sutton, Billy Danvers, Johnson Clark
Mildred Challenger's Holiday Highlights of 1956, with Sonny Farrar, Victor Dale, Fred Hugh, Joan and
Paul Sharratt, Terry Graves, Shirley Summers, Terence Delaney
(midnight matinee): The Show of All Shows, with stars of Gaytime (Playhouse), Trevor Brookes and his
Orchestra (Winter Gardens Pavilion), Vernon Adcock and his Orchestra (Rozel), Frivolities (Cove Pavil-
ion), Patricia Varley, John Harvey, Jay Martel, Leslie Sarony, Grand 'Miss Weston' Contest, in aid of
Bournville Church Building Appeal
December-January: Red Riding Hood, with Kathleen Warren, Sydney Barnes, Len Howe, Pat Fry, Rae
Croft, Eric Austin and Knightstone Orchestra

1957
April: Easter Parade, with Des O'Connor, Alice Dells, Reg Daponte and his Talking Racehorse, Lorna
Lee
June: Ernest Arnley and Gloria, George Bolton, Irving Kaye, Horler Twins
Leslie Adams, Rene Strange, Hilda Heath, Joan Hinde
For your Pleasure, with Tommy Fields, Kathleen and Ann Kemp, Shermans, Terry Sisters, Les Murphy,
Raoul
Laughter Parade, with Gladys Morgan and company
June-September: Gaytime, with Bob and Alf Pearson, Billy Baxter, Gwenda Wilkin, Burt Brooks with
'Harvey', Frank Hickey, Charles French, Dorothy Walker
December: Jack and the Beanstalk, with Helen James, Stanley Massey, Norman Griffin, Jack le White,
Billy Hooper

1958
April: New Airs and Faces, with Wyn Calvin, Diana Day, Barry and Julie Brooks, Alan Stilwell
For your Pleasure, with Johnny Dallas, Janette Fox, Elizabeth Gordon, Lane Twins, Aerial Kenways, John
Wade
May: Doctor in the House, with Geoffrey Hewitson's Famous Players - Peter Adamson, Laurie Adair,
Peter Hoyle, Walter Leybourne, Raymond Graham, Catherine Woodville
June-September: Gaytime, with Bob and Alf Pearson, Ken Roberts, Trio Vitalites (Jack Horton, Robert
Hargreaves, Janette Mayne), Anne Romaine, Freddie Harris, Valerie Gray, Arthur Downes, Brenda
Haydn, Terry Kendall
July-September: Sunday Showtime, with Ronnie Hancox and his Band, Susan Maughan
October: Western Theatre Ballet, with Brenda Last
December: Festival of Queens, with No 1 (Apprentice) Wing Pipe and Trumpet Band, RAF Locking,
Winthorpe Academy of Dancing pupils, in aid of National Children's Home

1959
March: Laughter Parade, with Bobbie Kimber, Vernon Sisters, Doreen Lane, John Guest, Ray Ravell
Bournemouth Symphony Orchestra, with Charles Groves
Mike it a Party, with The Four Jones Boys, Yvonne Ash, Les Madrigals, Vernon Sisters, Stan Waite
April: Fare Play, with Ken Haward, Rosemary Murray
May: See How they Run, with Geoffrey Hewitson's Famous Players - Peter Adamson, Phyllis Kenny, Jill
Simcox, Annette Hunt, Sid Lewis, Michael Barton, Colin Dando, Patricia Read, Ian Strachan, Susan Jameson
June-September: Gaytime, with Bob and Alf Pearson, Ken Roberts, Harry Haythorne, Sylvia Gray,
Ronald Maconaghie, Sylvia Ellis, Tony Manton, Brenda Haydn, Gwenda Wilkin, Terry Kendall

1960
April: The Merry Widow, with Weston-super-Mare Operatic Society - Raymond Miles, Lewis Stuckey,
Maureen James, Mervyn Evans, Charles Hawkins, Arthur Morris, Mary Underwood, Bill Leonard, Roy

Salmon, Leon Godby
June-October: Gaytime, with Bob and Alf Pearson, Ken Roberts, Gwenda Wilkin, Jean Anderson and Ronald Maconaghie, Jimmy Webster, Bernard Sharpe
October: Bournemouth Symphony Orchestra, with Alceo Galliera, Felix Kok
Ask me Another (BBC recording), with Franklin Englemann, Ted Moult, Olive Stephens, Dr Reginald Webster
December: Cinderella, with Georgina Rourke, Johnny Dallas, Shirley May, Colin Stowe, Charles Cardiff, Lee Allen, Rex Amos, Paul Waring, Douglas George's white ponies

1961

May: It's my Opinion (BBC recording), with Edward du Cann MP, Anthony Wedgwood Benn
May-September: Gaytime, with Ken Roberts, Four Jones Boys, Gwenda Wilkin, Christine Yates, Jeanette Given and Glen Marten, Graham James and Janet Don
July-August (Sundays): Joe 'Mr Piano' Henderson, Ken Dodd, Jimmy Young, Bryan Johnson, Lester Ferguson, Ronnie Hancox and his Band
November: British Legion Festival of Remembrance, with British Legion Silver Band, RAF Locking trumpeters, Don Charsley, Gwenda Wilkin, Lilian Bailey, Edward Deal, Jessica Hillman, in aid of Earl Haig Fund
December: Aladdin, with Rosemary Squires, Marcia Cross, Al Fuller and Janette, Tommy Elliott, Angela MacKenzie, Harry Orchid, George and Fred Eastwood

1962

January: Bournemouth Symphony Orchestra, with Myer Fredman, Roger Winfield
April: Bournemouth Symphony Orchestra, with Constantin Silvestri
The Royal Artillery Orchestra under Major SV Hays
June: Salad Days, with Peter Haddon Company - Roberta Huby, Richard Fraser, Paddy Glenn, Trevor Griffiths, Ben Aris
July-September: Let's Make a Night of It, with Beryl Reid, Billy Burden, Craig Douglas, Peter Walker, Jean and Peter Barbour, Julius Nehring
September: Salad Days, with Peter Haddon Company
December: Jack and the Beanstalk, with Reg 'Confidentially' Dixon, Toni Sinclair, Claire Wilson, Morris Parsons, Peter Ward, David Vickers

1963

April: Carousel, with Weston-super-Mare Operatic Society - John Groves, Judith Lane, Jeanne Hillman, Peter Brewer, Donald MacGregor, Olive Parsons, Doris Foreman, Annemarie Medland, Lewis Stuckey, Bill Leonard, Denise Frampton, Leon Godby, Tom Shearman
July-September: Let's Make a Night of It, with Terry Scott and Hugh Lloyd, Ronald Cryer and his Marionettes, Joe McBride, Jose Stewart, Terry Fearis, Elsye Monks
August: BBC Seaside Night radio recording, with Terry Scott and Hugh Lloyd, Charlie Chester, Lester Ferguson, Bert Weedon, Teddy Johnson and Pearl Carr
September: Those Were the Days, with Morris and Cowley, Harry Orchid, Trevor Morton, George and Fred Eastwood, Barbara Leeming, Paul Matthews, Tommy Elliott

1964

June: Those Were the Days, with Donald Peers, Marie Lloyd Junior, Morris and Cowley, Ravel, Harry Orchid, Leonard Sachs, Tom Mennard
July-September: Let's Make a Night of It, with Ivor Emmanuel, Lenny the Lion and Terry Hall, Patricia Bredin, Chris Carlsen, Robert Marlowe and Jenny Vance, Ken Flower
August (Sundays): Terry Scott and Hugh Lloyd, Adam Faith, The Roulettes, Jimmy Clitheroe, Joan Hinde, Freddie Frinton, Billy Burden

September: Gilbert and Sullivan for All, with D'Oyly Carte Opera principal soloists - Mary Sansom, Gillian Knight, David Palmer, Donald Adams, Weston-super-Mare Operatic Society chorus, William Cox-Ife
October: Arsenic and Old Lace, with Red Triangle Players - Mona Vickery, Joyce Brooks, Wilfred Fredricks, Peter Brewer, Lionel Calvin-Thomas, Joan Gibson, Michael Chew
December: Cinderella, with Bob and Alf Pearson, Chris Carlsen, Karan Simmons, Carole Mudie, Gene Anderton, April Varne, Elizabeth King, Clive Denham, Tony Stenson

1965
April: Junior Arts Festival
Brigadoon, with Weston-super-Mare Operatic Society - John Groves, Peter Brewer, Donald MacGregor, Nicholas Demirtges, Stan Bailey, John Tasker, Leslie A Scamp, Jeanne Hillman, Doris Foreman, Howard Simons, Lewis Stuckey, Denise Frampton, Annemarie Medland, Tom Shearman
The Man who Came to Dinner, with Weston-super-Mare Dramatic Society - Paul Dening, Brian Pike, David Hemming, Joyce Brooks, Mary Mee, Brian Morton-Hicks, Nan Hess
June-September: Let's Make a Night of It, with Ted Rogers, Mrs Mills, Chas McDevitt and Shirley Douglas, Peter Vernon, Bruce Allan, Bill Cameron, Tina Scott, Ken Flower and his Music
November: Hiawatha, with Rossholme School, in aid of British Red Cross Society and Mayor's Christmas Appeal
December: Red Riding Hood and the Wicked Wolf, with Sheila Buxton, Len Howe, Jeanette Coles, Fran Parsons, Bobo Rexano, Morris Parsons, Tommy Elliott

1966
May: The Amorous Prawn, with Weston-super-Mare Dramatic Society - Joy Wilkinson, David Hemming, Tony Hayman, Brian Pike, Brian Morton-Hicks, Neville Redman, Lesley Fear, Jenny Hillman, Michael Usher, Gregory Thacker
Cat on the Fiddle, with Wayfarers Drama Group - Brenda White, Ian Gibson, Mary Chubb, Russell Fear, Dorothy MacDowell, Lawrence Gillard, Gwen Watson, Brian Weston, Peter Magor, Constance Seedhouse, Ernest Gibson
Son of Oblomov, with Bill Kerr, Valerie van Ost, Barbara Whatley, David Lloyd Meredith, Charles Vance
Clarkie's Casserole, with Clarkson Rose, Bob and Alf Pearson, Randolph Sutton, Margery Manners, Chris Carlsen, Faust and Valerie, Terry Doogan
June: Carry on Father, with Ken Platt, Sylvia Melville, Laurie Davey, Roy Barraclough, Olga Bennett, Peter Greene, Hugh Kealy, Diana Irwin
June-September: The Norman Vaughan Show, with Norman Vaughan, Karlins, Frankie Holmes, Betty Smith Quintet, Vivienne George, Rod King
December: Aladdin, with Arthur English, Vicki Lane, Shirley May, Douglas Charlton, Don Maclean, Harry Orchid

1967
March: Guys and Dolls, with Weston-super-Mare Operatic Society - John Collings, Michael Edwards, Jeanne Hillman, Brinley James, Nesta Shearman, Brian Morton-Hicks, Bill Clout, Peter Brewer
May: Home this Afternoon BBC recording, with Derek Jones, Stan Stennett, Barbara Buchanan, Kenneth Hudson, Jeremy Carrad
Clarkie's Casserole, with Clarkson Rose, Adelaide Hall, Frankie Holmes, Barry Johns, El Granadas, Lila and her Dogs
June: Starnite Spectacular, with Billy Whittaker and Mimi Law, Three Squires, Judith Stubbs, Melita Manger
June-September: The Fol-de-Rols, with Freddie Sales, Howell Evans, Patricia Kane, Jennifer Toye, Brian Edwards, Freddie Eldrett
October: Autumn Comedy Playhouse: Busybody, Love Locked Out, Fools Rush In, with Velvey Attwood, Nicholas Brent, Edward Granville, Patricia Temple, Alan Corser, Ian Cunningham, Vanessa Riches, Norma Streader, Rosalind Harbinson

November: The Sooty 1968 Talent Show, with Harry Corbett
December: Dick Whittington and his Cat, with Vince and Rita Starr, Jean Tyler, Louis Roberts, Calvin Kaye, Gordon Holdom

1968
March: Gilbert and Sullivan for All, with D'Oyly Carte Opera Company soloists Valerie Masterton, Donald Adams, Phillip Potter, Helen Landis, and Jessica Hillman, Tom Shearman
Harlequin Ballet, with Jacqui Tallis, Donald McAlpine, Barbara Vernon, Serge Ivanov, Paul Benson, Suzi Edwards, Patsy Urquhart, Marie Lavell
Bunny Baron's Palace of Varieties, with Reg Dixon, Penny Nicholls, Alec Pleon, Gwen Overton and Clive Stock, Henri Vadden and Lady, Alan Beale, Toni and Terry Calder, Raymond Paul and his Music
Just the Ticket, with Charlie Chester, Chili Bouchier
June-September: The Fols '68, with Denny Willis, Ronnie Collis, Judy Bowen, Johnny Mack, Rosalind Roberts, Paul Matthews, Michael John, Sandra Wrennall
December: Oliver!, with Rossholme School, in aid of Church of England's Children's Society
Robin Hood and his Merry Men, with Len Howe, Nick Nissen, Margaret Moore

1969
April: My Fair Lady, with Weston-super-Mare Operatic Society - Nesta Shearman, Brian Canniford, Don MacGregor, Stanley Bailey, Heather Collings, Fred Burrows, Lilian Bailey, Barbara Gray
Junior Arts Festival
The Rivals, with Red Triangle Players - Andrew Walker, Frances Urwin, Dennis Coote, Francis Maddocks, Barbara Usher, Christopher Lambert
The Diary of Anne Frank, with The College Players - Lisa Potter, Peter Wilde Parsons, Peter Nicholls, Gillian Hunt
May: Hay Fever, with Weston-super-Mare Dramatic Society - Mary Mee, Clive Darke, Joan Townsend, Ray Edbrooke, Terry Street, Nina Rees, Tony Hayman, Mary Edbrooke, Joan Fisher
Quiet Weekend, with Wayfarers Drama Group - Constance Seedhouse, Phyllis Cooksley, Ernest Gibson, Ian Gilroy, Dorothy Sarsfield, Linda Connett, Betty Board, Eileen Higginbottom, Lawrence Gillard, Gwen Watson, Phyllis Moon
The Lodger, The Edge of Fear, with Charles Vance company - Valentine Dyall, Kay Woodman, Clive Cable, Christy Carroll, Bob Blacklock, Hugh Myatt, Michael Jenkins, Rosalyn Slater
June-September: Let's all Go to the Music Hall, with Sandy Powell, Peter Cavanagh, Cavan O'Connor, Margery Manners, Eddie Reindeer, Angelo and Lee, Vernon Sisters, Dom and Josie, Maurice Bromley

1970
June-September: Summer Showboat, with Tony Mercer, Alton Douglas, Roy Earl, Lawrie Adam, Mike North and Sheila West, Vicki Lane, Douglas Charlton, Glam Twins, Pamela Burn Glam Dancers, Vernon Jones, Philip Charles, Tom Harvey

1971
June-September: Summer Showboat, with Pearl Carr and Teddy Johnson, Frankie Holmes, Alan Beale, Martin and Sylvia Konyot, Nicky Healey, Michael John, Alan Tirrell Trio

1972
June-September: Summer Showboat, with Barry Kent, Derek Roy, Nigel Hopkins, Desmond King, Jackie Joy and Bill Ryan, Jackie Baker, Janice Armstrong, Les Brown and his Music

1973
June-September: Summer Showboat, with Bobby Dennis, Benny Garcia, Syd Wright, Michael Tye-Walker and Corinne, Virginia Drinkwater, Janice Armstrong, Les Brown and his Music

1974
June-September: Summer Showboat, with Reg 'Confidentially' Dixon, Ravel, Bonnie Downs, Barry Hopkins, Vicki Lane and Douglas Charlton, Louis Roberts, Austen Simmonds, Tom Harvey, Alistair Hinton and his Music

1975
June-September: Cabaret Showtime, with Pearl Carr and Teddy Johnson, Syd Wright, Les Wilson, Chris Booth and Cathy Houghton, Don Phillips and his Music

1976
June-September: Cabaret Showtime, with Dai Francis, Frankie Holmes, Michelle and Myles, Bobby Bragg, Karan Simmons, Don Phillips and his Music

1977
June-September: Cabaret Showtime, with Millican and Nesbitt, Johnny Stewart, Mel and Pam Wingfield, Jon and Janette, Don Phillips and his Music

1978
June-September: Cabaret Showtime, with Los Zafiros, Van Buren and Greta, Patton Brothers, Jackie Kelly, Satin Bells, Don Phillips and his Music

1979
June-September: The Bernie Clifton Show, with Bernie Clifton, Len Lowe, Bobby Crush, Rusty Goffe, Valentine, Lisa Gaye Dancers, Brian Farley and his Music

1980
June-September: Mondays to Wednesdays: The Vernon Adcock Music Show, with Semprini, Christine Campbell, Peter Lewis, Roger Green, Helen Rangeley, Vernon Adcock Orchestra. *Thursdays to Saturdays:* The Good Olde Days
July and August Sundays: Best o' Brass, with Sun Life Stanshawe Band, The Cory Band, William Davis Construction Group Band, Wingates Temperance Band, Desford Colliery Welfare Band, Yorkley Onward Band, The Great Universal Band, Camborne Town Band, City of Coventry Band

1981
June-September: Mondays to Wednesdays: The Vernon Adcock Music Show, with John Hanson, Christine Campbell, Peter Lewis, Karl Rainer, Helen Rangeley, Vernon Adcock Orchestra. *Thursdays to Saturdays:* The Good Olde Days
July and August Sundays: Champions of Brass, with Sun Life Stanshawe Band, St Austell Band, Hymac Rhymney Band, William Davis Construction Group Band, Camborne Town Band

1982
June-September: Vernon Adcock's Wonderful World of Music, with Karl Rainer, Peter Lewis, Christine Campbell, Cindy Foster, Vernon Adcock Orchestra
July and August Sundays: Champions of Brass/Holiday for Brass, with Cinderford Band, Yorkley Onward Band, Sun Life Stanshawe Band, St Austell Band, Mid-Rhondda Band, Roberts Bakery Band, Yorkley Onward Band, Tredegar Workmen's Band

1983
May-October: The Organist Entertains, with John King, Ivan Cottrell, Philip Rogerson, Don Hammond Rollermania Entertainments roller disco
Snooker competition with Steve Davis

1984
May-September: The Organist Entertains, with Alan Cox, Philip Rogerson
Rollermania Entertainments roller disco
June: Snooker competition with Steve Davis
September: Scooter rally convention

1985
May-September: The Organist Entertains, with Alan Cox, Philip Rogerson
Sequence and ballroom dancing
September: Scooter rally convention

1986
May-September: The Organist Entertains, with Alan Cox, Philip Rogerson
Sequence and ballroom dancing

1987
January: Geno Washington and the Ram Jam Band
February: Chesterfields, Flatmates
Brilliant Corners, Chorchazade
Blue Aeroplanes
Steve Marriott and the Official Receivers
March: Desmond Dekker and the Aces
Mighty Mighty
Georgie Fame and the Blue Flames
April: The Bodines, Blue Train
Geno Washington and the Ram Jam Band, Rhythm Party
Black Roots, Rodney Allen
George Melly, John Chilton's Feetwarmers
May: Camper Van Beethoven
The Fall
Tygers of Pan Tang
June-October: The Organist Entertains, with Alan Cox
Sequence dancing with Ted Burroughs
June: Mud
Love Affair
July: Marmalade
Rockin' Tony and the Sidewinders
August: The Searchers
The Tremeloes
The Baldettes
The Sweet
September: Mungo Jerry
Rock for Ages, with Renegade Flight, Claytown Troupe, March of Time, The Chalk Garden, in aid of
Magic Me project
October: Renegade Flight, The Long March
Ballroom dancing, with Raymond Kaye Orchestra
November: Attila the Stockbroker, The Ruin
December: Renegade Flight

1988
January: Victorian Night, with Weston Lions, TOPPS Drama Club, in aid of local children's charities

Renegade Flight
Exercise Yard, Flair, in aid of cot death support and research
April: Losenges Soul Review, Fingertips
June: Beside the Seaside, with TOPPS Drama Club
June-September: The Organist Entertains
July: Rikky T, The Pete Richards Roadshow
Winston
Giraffe
Benny Bright Orchestra
August: City Dread, Israeli Movement
Love Affair
Ice Hot
Jet Harris, Tangent
Mark Brothers Blues Band
September: Jacuzzi
Music Hall, with West Woodspring Inner Wheel Club, in aid of British Heart Foundation
Cry Paradise, High Tide

1989
February: Valentine's dance, with HM Royal Marine Dance Band
Summer: Lunchtime organist
Sequence dancing with Ted Burroughs
Runn Runn Disco
Evenings of Entertainment, with Dave Linsen at the organ
Gordon Roger Duo
The Organist Entertains, with Neil Eyre
August: Dave Terry Band
Love Affair

1990
January: Weston Youth Orchestra
Summer: Bavarian Nights, with Karl Wilheim Oom Pah Band
That'll be the Day, with Fizzical, Paul Da Vinci, Ritz, Gary Anderson
All-Star Wrestling
Sequence and ballroom dancing
Sixties Nights, with Brian Poole and the Electrix, The Dreamers, Vanity Fair, Fourmost, Dave Berry and the Cruisers, Cupid's Inspiration, The Dooleys, Love Affair, Applejacks
Summer Showtime, with The Wurzels, The Mad Hatters, The Brother Lees
Comedy Night Specials, with John Dolly, Darren Day, Two Tone; Kenny Smiles, Kevin Devane, Mike Jerome, Johnny Walker, Julie Thursday Duo

1991
Sundays: ballroom dancing

Weston-super-Mare Operatic Society

1909 The Pirates of Penzance
1910 The Gondoliers
1911 (April and September) Merrie England
1912 Princess Ida
1913 The Yeomen of the Guard
1914 The Mikado
1920 Dorothy
1921 The Gondoliers
1922 The Mikado
1923 The Yeomen of the Guard
1924 San Toy
1925 A Country Girl
1926 Florodora
1927 HMS Pinafore/Trial by Jury
1928 The Quaker Girl
1929 The Toreador
1930 The Rose of Araby
1931 Merrie England
1932 The Vagabond King
1933 The Gondoliers
1934 The Pirates of Penzance
1935 The Yeomen of the Guard
1936 The Maid of the Mountains
1937 The Rebel Maid
1938 The Arcadians
1939 The Mikado
1940 Iolanthe
1947 The Gondoliers

1948 The Mikado
1949 A Country Girl
1950 Rose Marie
1951 The Yeomen of the Guard
1952 The Desert Song
1952 Merrie England
1953 Chu Chin Chow
1954 HMS Pinafore/Trial by Jury
1955 The Quaker Girl
1956 Call Me Madam
1957 White Horse Inn
1958 The New Moon
1959 Oklahoma!
1960 The Merry Widow
1961 South Pacific
1962 Annie Get your Gun
1963 Carousel
1964 Showboat
1964 The Yeomen of the Guard
1965 Brigadoon
1965 The Pirates of Penzance
1966 The Pajama Game
1966 Trial by Jury/HMS Pinafore
1967 Guys and Dolls
1967 La Belle Helene
1968 Kiss Me Kate
1968 Die Fledermaus
1969 My Fair Lady

Weston-super-Mare Dramatic Society

1918 The Private Secretary
1919 What Happened to Jones
1922 The Perfect Lover
1923 The Chinese Puzzle
1924 The Thirteenth Chair
1925 Trelawny of the Wells
1926 Diplomacy
1927 Other People's Worries
1928 Mr Wu
1929 The Lilies of the Field
1930 The Barton Mystery
1931 A Cuckoo in the Nest
1932 Ebb Tide/Cupboard Love/Shadow/
    The Man in the Bowler Hat
1932 The Dover Road/Interference
1933 Exit/The Bride/Shanghai/Not Classified
1933 Bird in Hand
1934 Monsieur Beaucaire
1935 Autumn Crocus
1936 The Ghost Train
1937 Full House
1938 Pride and Prejudice
1944 Jupiter Laughs
1945 Quiet Wedding
1945 The Breadwinner
1946 Call It a Day
1946 The Importance of Being Earnest

1947 To Kill a Cat
1947 The Rose Without a Thorn
1948 Grand National Night
1948 No Medals
1949 The Venetian
1949 The Man from the Ministry
1950 Dear Octopus
1950 The Rivals
1951 On Monday Next
1951 Pink String and Sealing Wax
1952 The Circle/Tanner
1953 Peter Pan
1953 The Gioconda Smile
1954 Home and Beauty
1955 Peter Pan
1955 The Hollow
1956 St Joan
1964 Sabrina Fair
1965 The Man who Came to Dinner
1965 Charley's Aunt
1966 The Amorous Prawn
1966 Murder at the Vicarage
1967 The Imaginary Invalid
1967 The Love of Four Colonels
1968 Pride and Prejudice
1968 All Things Bright and Beautiful
1969 Hay Fever

British Legion pantomimes

1934 Babes in the Wood
1935 Robinson Crusoe
1936 Aladdin and his Wonderful Lamp
1937 Cinderella
1938 Dick Whittington
1939 Mother Goose
1945 Cinderella
1946 Jack and the Beanstalk
1947 Robinson Crusoe
1948 Babes in the Wood
1949 Aladdin
1950 Red Riding Hood
1951 Dick Whittington and his Cat
1952 Cinderella
1953 Jack and the Beanstalk
1954 Sinbad the Sailor
1955 Little Miss Muffet
1956 Robinson Crusoe
1958 Babes in the Wood

Acknowledgements

I am grateful to the following for their help with this book:

Brian Austin, Tansin Benn, Chris Carlsen, Colin Charsley, Terry Counsell, Shirley Dimoline, James Fredricks, John Fursland, Viona Lane, Pete Magor, Tom O'Connor, Sharon Poole, Brenda Thompson, Colin Tyler, Lauri Williams, Doris Wilsher, The British Music Hall Society and the staff of Weston-super-Mare Library's Frederick Wood Room.

Julie Andrews, Robert Windeler (WH Allen, 1982)

Picture credits

Cover and pages 40, 88, 110 (bottom) and 120: North Somerset Council and Somerset County Council Heritage Service; page 4: Old-Maps.co.uk and Ordnance Survey; pages 9, 14, 21, 27, 28, 44, 46, 52, 54, 91,128 and 145: Weston-super-Mare Library, North Somerset Council; page 18: The British Library; pages 33, 34 and 65: James Fredricks; page 39: ©English Heritage. Licensor www.rcahms.gov.uk; page 43: John Fursland; pages 56 (top left and bottom right), 58, 79 and 80: Brenda Thompson; pages 56 (bottom left) and 57: The Magic Circle; pages 60 and 61: Colin Charsley; pages 83 and 84: Shirley Dimoline; pages 89, 102, 105, 106, 112, 115, 119, 123 and 142: Courtesy of *Weston Mercury*; page 94 (bottom): The British Music Hall Society; pages 96 and 148: Tom O'Connor - raetoc.com; page 101: Leslie G Sandys; page 108: Lauri Williams; page 110 (top): Chris Carlsen; page 118: Bamforth and Co, Yorkshire; page 124: South West Heritage Trust and Somerset Archives and Local Studies; page 127: Garth D Smith; page 132: *The Stage*; pages 136 and 137: Old Theatres magazine – www.oldtheatres.co.uk

Index

Adams, Donald 113, 121
Adamson, Peter 95
Adcock, Vernon 103, 121, 134-138
Addicott, Charles 13
Aladdin 100, 118, 119, 149
Albani, Emma 18
Alexander, Gerald 37-41, 45, 46
Alexander, Joline 88, 90
Alexander, Judythe 68, 88
Alexander, Scott 23
Alexander School of Dancing 88, 114
Alexandra Gardens 32, 126
Alexandra Players 111
All-Star Sunday Concerts 111
Allan, Mozart 59
Ambrose 49
Anderson, Jean 99
Andrews, Julie 71
Andrews, Ted and Barbara 71
Archers, The 88
Arena Theatre 78
Arts Council of Great Britain 69
Ash, Robert 93
Ask Me Another 100
Asquith, Earl of Oxford and 23
Assembly Rooms, High Street 17
Attlee, Clement 55
Austin, Brian 131
Austin, Eric 87
Austen, Jane 24

Babes in the Wood 70, 82, 86, 91, 95
Bachelors, The 107
Baedeker raid 44, 63, 64
Bailey, Lilian 100
Bailey, Stan 123
Ballet Rambert 69, 105
Bannister Howard, J 29
Baring Brothers 17
Barnes, Sydney 51, 56, 58, 66, 78-81, 85, 91
Baron, Bunny 100, 107, 113, 114, 126, 132
Barrett, Philip 90
Bath, 6th Marquess of 104, 105

Baxter, Billy 93
Beatles, The 107
Beauty Jungle, The 103
Benn, Tansin 114, 115
Bennett, Billy 57
Bennett, Christine 57, 66
Benson, Bernard 64, 66
Benson, Sir Frank 5
Bere, Frank 43
Bernie Clifton Show, The 133, 134
Beside the Seaside 140
Bird, William 38
Birneck Pier 5, 11, 12, 134, 143, 144, 147
Black and White Minstrel Show, The 126, 129
Bond, Stanley 68
Bonn, Issy 68, 69
Bosley, George 51, 52, 54, 56, 57, 62, 63, 70, 80, 84, 91
Boswell's Royal Circus 42
Boulevard Congregational Church 105, 106
Bournemouth Symphony Orchestra 95
Boyden, Rev William 11, 13
Bredin, Patricia 111, 112
Brewer, Peter 123
Bristol Old Vic Company 69
British Legion 42, 46, 52, 61, 67, 68, 82, 84, 86-88, 95
British Legion Festival of Remembrance 100
Britton, Tony 63-65
Broomfield, Harry 35
Brother Lees, The 142
Brough and 'Archie Andrews', Peter 75
Brown, Harold 35
Brown, Lawrence 45
Brown, Suzy 135
Brown, Teddy 45
Bryant, Eddie 20
BS Group/Gaming International 145-149
Burden, Billy 101, 103
Burgess, HC (Harry) 31, 36, 53, 59
Burroughs, Ted and Sue 140
Butt, Dame Clara 5, 18, 44
Butt, Henry 50

Butter, Barnabas 35
By Candlelight 83
Byles, Beryl and Reg 82
Byng, Douglas 69

Cabaret Showtime 129-131
Café de Paris 58, 59
Call Me Madam 89, 107
Calvin, Wyn 81, 85, 86, 100
Campbell, Christine 135
Carl Rosa Opera 16
Carlsen, Chris 110, 111, 113
Carmo, The Great 42
Carousel 104
Carr, Pearl 106, 127, 129, 150
Caruso, Enrico 38
Casino Girl, The 18
Cavanagh, Peter 74, 125
CEMA (Council for the Encouragement of
        Music and Arts) 69
Central Picture House 34, 39, 104
Chamberlain, Neville 59
Chamberlain Hall 77
Chapman, Constance 57, 111
Charsley, Chris 60, 61
Charsley, Colin 71, 73, 87
Charsley, Don 61, 87
Chesney, Ronald 77
Chester, Charlie 106
Chevalier, Maurice 129
Churchill, Sarah 55
Cinderella 83, 113, 114
Clark, John 90
Clark, Johnson 91
Claxton, Hedley 93, 95-97
Cleese, John 73
Clifford Essex Band 36
Clifton, Bernie 132, 133
Clitheroe, Jimmy 112
Cole, Lieutenant Walter 20
Coliseum, London 55, 81
College Players, The 111, 113
Collings, Heather 109, 111

Connor, Kenneth 69
Conway, Russ 103
Corbett, Harry 120
Cork and Orrey, Earl of 15
Cotton, Billy 74
Counsell, Terry 81, 93
Courage (brewer) 138, 139
Cox, Alan 138
Cox-Ife, William 121
Crazy Days 55
Crockford-Hawley, John 138, 148
Croft, David 106
Cross, Jack 38
Crowther, Leslie 126
Crush, Bobby 132, 133
Cryer, Ronald 105

Dane, Della 34
Dane, Wilfrid 34
Dankworth, Johnny 103
Danvers, Billy 91
Datas 37
David Garrick 18
Davies, Sir Walford 41
Davis, Joe 138
Davis, Steve 138, 139
de Savary, Peter 141, 143
Deal, Edward 100
Dekker and the Aces, Desmond 140
Dennis, Bobby 128
Denville Players 36
Dick Whittington and his Cat 83, 90
Dickie, Mary 105
Dietrich, Marlene 45
Digby-Smith, Elizabeth 90
Dimoline, Eunice 83, 86
Dimoline, Iris 86
Dimoline, Marjorie 83, 86
Dimoline, Rosina 83, 86
Dimoline, Victor 52, 84, 86
Dimo-Panto Company 83, 84, 86
Dixon, Reg 'Confidentially' 81, 104, 129
Dodd, Ken 73, 100

Dolly Sisters, The 107
Dors, Diana 77
Dossor, Harry Arthur 31
Douglas, Alton 126
Douglas, Craig 103
Douglas, Shirley 117
Dowler, Cyril 64
Downes, Arthur 93
Downs, Bonnie 129
D'Oyly Carte, Helen 20, 24
Driver, Betty 74
Duncan and his Blue Grass Boys, Johnny 95
Dyall, Valentine 125

Eager, Frank 88
Earl, Roy 126
Edbrooke, Ray 150
Edge of Fear, The 113, 125
Educating Archie 75
Edward VII 15, 17, 23
Electric Moving Pictures 17, 23, 26
Electric Theatre 28
Ellington, Ray 95
Elliott GH 91
Emmanuel, Ivor 110-112
Engelmann, Franklin 100
English, Arthur 118
English Heritage 144
English Tourist Board 134, 139
ENSA (Entertainments National Service
        Association) 62, 100
Environment, Department of 144
Equity 113
European Community Single Regeneration
        Budget 145
Evans, Captain Teddy 32

Faith, Adam 111, 112
Fame and the Blue Flames, Georgie 139
Fascists, British Union of 23
Fearis, Terry 105
Feldman, Marty 73
Field and Wilkins 74

Fields, Gracie 38, 52, 58
Fields, Tommy 69
Flavell, Basil 113, 120, 121, 126, 129, 130, 132
Flavell, Robert 113
Fletcher, Cyril 74, 81
Florence, Mademoiselle 20
Florodora 18
Fol-de-Rols, The 119, 120
Foreman, Doris (see Doris Wilsher)
Formby, Frank 64
Fortescue, Frank 52
Four Jones Boys, The 99
Fox, Dr Edward Long 10, 141, 149
Fox, Francis 10
Francis, Dai 129-131
Frankau, Ronald 78
Franklin, Gretchen 55, 88
Franklyn, Leo 126
Fredman, Myer 95
Fredricks, Carlton 33, 34, 65, 66
Fredricks, James 66
Fredricks senior, James 33, 34, 65, 66, 70, 85
Fredricks, Leo 33, 34
Fredricks, Wilfred 33, 34, 65, 66, 107, 108, 111
Frinton, Freddie 112
Frivolities 78
Frost, David 107
Fuller, Leslie 64
Fursland, Leslie J 24, 43

Galliera, Alceo 95
Gammons, Reginald 48, 51
Gaye, Lisa 114, 119, 132, 133
Gaytime 6, 93, 94, 96, 97, 99-101, 116, 117
Geoffrey Hewitson's Famous Players 95
George, HRH Prince 42, 44
George and Margaret 55
Gerald Alexander Repertory Company 45
Gerry and the Pacemakers 107
Ghost Train, The 24
Gigli, Beniamino 38
Gilmour, Sally 69
Glentworth Bay 11, 12, 38

Godby, Francis 35, 36
Godby, Leon 87
Godfrey's Troubadour Follies, Will 75
Goffe, Rusty 133
Goodyear, Wyn 82
Goolden, Richard 55
Grand Atlantic Hotel 23, 117
Grand Pier 6, 11-13, 17, 21, 30, 35, 41, 75, 86, 103, 137
Graves, David 70, 85
Gray, Valerie 93
Great Western Railway 17, 24, 41
Green, Roger 135
Grey, Viscount 23
Grey-Burnand, Edith 16
Griffiths, Peter 108
Grinfield, Charles (CT) 18, 20, 24, 32
Grosvenor Orchestra 14, 16, 18
Grove Park and Pavilion 34, 42, 50, 53, 54, 58, 59, 63
Groves, Charles 95

Haddon, Peter 103
Haldane, Lord 29
Hall, Adelaide 78
Hall, Henry 58
Hall and 'Lenny the Lion', Terry 110-112
Hancox, Ronnie 97, 99, 100
Hanson, John 135
Hare, Robertson 30
Harris, Roger 134
Harrison, Rex 41, 97
Harry Hanson's Court Players 78
Hay, George 51, 53, 54, 56, 59, 62, 64, 66, 70, 71, 73, 75, 78, 80, 81, 85, 87, 89-91
Hay, Joan 48
Hay Junior, Will 48
Hay Fever 57, 111
Heap, Benjamin 15, 16
Hello, America 64
Henderson, Joe 'Mr Piano' 100
Henlere, Herschel 78
Hicks and his Cabin Boys, Colin 95

Hillman, Jessica 87, 90, 100, 121
Hippodrome, Bedminster 55
Hippodrome, Bristol 45, 53, 74
Hippodrome/The Talk of the Town, London 121
Holloway, Stanley 57
Holmes, Frankie 118, 128
Home Guard 63, 70
Hopkins, Barry 129
Howe, Len 115
Howerd, Frankie 6, 73, 77
Hugh and I 106
Hughes, David 99
Hughes, Rex 82
Hurst, George 95
Hutchinson, Leslie A (Hutch) 73, 78
Hutton Moor Leisure Centre 141
Hylton's Carlton Band, Jack 38

Importance of Being Earnest, The 57
Inman, John 125
Inter-Allied Variety Week 64
It's That Man Again 70

Jack and the Beanstalk 75, 84, 95, 104
Jackson, Clive 135, 139, 140
Jackson, William 52, 53
Jackson-Barstow, John Jeremiah 10
James, Brynley 123
James, Doreen 54, 114
James, Mavis 54, 114
Jamieson, Jean 111
Jane Eyre 89
Jefferies, Tom 18
Jenkins, Jean 149
Jenny Villiers 69
Johnson, Bryan 100
Johnson and his West Indian Orchestra, Ken 'Snakehips' 59
Johnson, Teddy 106, 127, 129, 150
Jones, Bill 18
Joyce, William (Lord Haw-Haw) 23, 24
Junior Arts Festival 113-114

Kearton, Cherry 37
Kendall, Kay 96
Kendall, Terry 96
Kent, Barry 128
Kenway, Nan 74, 80
Kerr, Bill 125
Kiddie, Nor 64
Kimber and 'Augustus Peabody', Bobbie 75
King, Hetty 91
King, John 138
Kingfisher Leisure 141-143
Kinsey, Lemuel 87
Knight, Gillian 113
Knightstone Leisure Ltd 143
Knightstone Singers' and Dancers' Club 140, 142
Konyot, Martin and Sylvia 128
Korris, Harry 69
Krauss and Son, A 13
Kubelik, Jan 41
Kunz, Charlie 48

Lacey, Ken 147
Ladies in Review 65
Lady, Meet the Navy 64
Landis, Helen 121
Lane, Gordon 51, 53, 54, 56, 59, 62, 66, 69, 70, 78, 80, 81, 91
Lane, Kathleen 66
Lane, Raymond 81
Latter, George 47
Laurel and Hardy 77, 129
Laye, Evelyn 57
Leaver James, 19, 32
Let Sleeping Wives Lie 126
Let's All Go to the Music Hall 125, 127
Let's Make a Night of It 6, 100-102, 104-106, 110, 111, 116-118
Lever, Al 50
Lewis, Peter 135
Lindfield, TE 50
Little Lord Fauntleroy 18
Lloyd, Hugh 102, 104, 105, 111

Lloyd George, David 23
Local Government Board 11, 29
Locke, George 87
Lord Chamberlain 67, 69
Los Zafiros 130, 131
Loss, Joe 49
Love in the Mist 66
Lowe, Len 132-134
Lucan, Arthur 74
Lupino family 55
Luzita, Sara 69

Macari and his Dutch Serenaders 74
Maclean, Don 119
Maconaghie, Ronald 99
Mad Hatters, The 142
Magic Circle, The 51
Magor, Pete 83
Maid of the Mountains, The 30
Make Mine Music 99
Manners, Margery 125
Marconi, Guglielmo 15
Marine Lake 38, 39, 90, 93, 101, 121, 134, 137-139, 143, 145, 146
Marriott, Steve 139
Masterton, Valerie 121
Maughan, Susan 97
Mavdor dancers/Mavdor School of Dancing 54, 114, 149
May, Shirley 119
Mayerl, Billy 55
McBride, Joe 105
McDevitt, Chas 117
McShane, Kitty 74
Melly, George 139
Melrose Café 51, 84, 90
Menary, Anthony 119
Mendelssohn and his Hawaiian Serenaders, Felix 74
Menuhin, Yehudi 38
Mercer, Tony 126, 129
Middleton, Caspar 48-51, 53
Miles, Michael 74

Miller, Max 6, 73
Millican and Nesbitt 130
Millier, HG 38, 55
Mills, Mrs (Gladys) 117
Millward and the Nitwits, Sid 73
Modern Venus Beauty Competition 77, 78, 98, 105, 126, 138
Mogg's Military Prize Band 28, 29, 32, 35
Monks, Elsye 105
Morecambe and Wise 6, 73
Moreton, Robert 73
Morgan, Gladys 103
Mosley, Sir Oswald 23
Mother Goose 83
Moult, Ted 100
Murdoch, Richard 74
Murray, Paul 55, 59, 62
My Fair Lady 108, 122, 123, 125

NAAFI (Navy, Army and Air Force Institutes) 62
Neilson-Terry, Phyllis 55
Nell Gwyn 18
New Airs and Faces 100
Newman, Bernard 59
Nicholls, Sue 125
Nights of Gladness 64
Norman, Norman V 18
North Somerset Council 145, 148, 149
Norton Thompson, Rev Preb B 32
Norville, Bert 18, 32

O'Brian, Frank 64, 78
O'Connor, Cavan 125
O'Connor, Des 92
O'Connor, Tom 96
Odd Man In 113
Odeon Cinema 45, 65, 77, 95, 103, 104, 107, 141
Oklahoma! 107, 111
Old King Cole 85, 86
Oldmixon Players 69
Organ, G and M 48

Organist Entertains, The 138, 139
Out of the Blue 48, 71
Out of the Hat 53

Pajama Game, The 109
Palace Theatre 34, 39
Palmer, David 107, 113
Passmore Brothers 70
Pathé's Weekly Animated Gazette 28
Patton Brothers 130
Paul, Raymond 96, 99
Payne, William 15, 17, 22, 25, 32, 35, 38
Peel, Viscount 23
Pearson, Bob and Alf 93, 94, 96-99, 113, 150
Perrett, Billy 8
Peter Pan 111
Philip, the Duke of Edinburgh, HRH Prince 74, 129, 149
Playhouse Theatre 78, 84, 92, 93, 100, 103, 107, 113, 114, 117, 122, 125, 126, 130, 134, 137, 138, 149, 150
Pleasence, Donald 66, 68
Pollard, HW 13
Pool, The 77, 98, 134, 138, 147
Poole's Myriorama 21, 22
Potter, Phillip 121
Powell, Leslie 87
Powell, Sandy 68, 122, 125, 127
Preager and his Broadcasting Band, Lou 48
Price, Monty 52
Pride and Prejudice 24
Priestley, JB 69
Prince's Theatre, Bristol 46
Private Secretary, The 24
Puss in Boots 76, 84

The Queen, Elizabeth II, HM 77, 149
Queen of Hearts 79, 85
Quiet Wedding 64
Quiet Weekend 125

RAF Locking 59, 100, 107
Rainer, Karl 135, 138

Ravel (Alfred Vorzanger) 129
Raymond, Miriam 66
Read, Al 107
Red Cross, British 30
Red Riding Hood 86
Red Triangle Players 40, 89, 107, 111, 113, 126
Redgrave, Angela 90
Redgrave, John 90, 122, 149
Redgrave, Lynn 90
Redrow Homes 149
Reed, Andrew 105
Regent Picture House/Gaumont cinema 34, 39, 104, 126
Reid, Beryl 68, 101, 103
Reindeer, Eddie 125, 127
Rix, Brian 122, 126
Robbins, Bertie 79
Roberts, Ken 96, 97, 99
Robertson, James 95
Robeson, Paul 5, 45
Robey, George 50
Robin Hood and his Merry Men 122
Robinson, Douglas 'Cardew' 73
Robinson Crusoe 48, 68, 88
Roe, Wilfred 52, 83, 86, 87
Rogers, Ted 117
Rogers' Field 11
Rolland, Roy 74
Rollermania Entertainments 138, 142
Ronalde, Ronnie 75, 77, 81
Rookery Nook 69
Rose, Clarkson 70
Roulettes, The 112
Roy, Derek 128
Royal Institute of British Architects 13
Rozel, The (hotel) 147
Rozel Bandstand/Sun Lounge and Café 62, 99, 103, 121, 137, 138, 147
Rumford, Kennerley 44
Rushworth J 28

Saint Joan 57
Salberg, Keith 89

Sales, Freddie 120
San Toy 18
Sanatorium, Royal West of England 11
Sanderson, Chris 143-145
Sands, Leslie 140
Sandys, Captain George 29
Sansom, Mary 113
Scamp, Leslie 89, 107
Schooling, Elisabeth 69
Scott, Terry 102, 104, 105, 107, 111, 117
Searchers, The 139
Seaside Night 103, 106
Secombe, Harry 81
Semprini 134
Shackleton, Sir Ernest 32
Shallish, Tansin (see Tansin Benn)
Shearman, Tom 108, 109, 122
Shields, Ella 73
Shilling Sunday Popular Concerts 49, 50
Shining Hour, The 57
Shorney, Jesse 5
Show of Shows, The 48-51
Showboat 107, 111
Shrimpton, Bert 73
Silvestri, Constantin 95
Simmons, Karan 115, 149, 150
Six-Five Special 95
Sleeping Beauty, The 61, 67
Smedley, Lillian 81
Smith, Betty 118
Smith, Gipsy Pat 22
Smith, Harold 18
Smith, Dr Howard 148
Smith, Jessie 81
Smith, Les 132
Smyth-Pigott, Cecil Hugh 10
Son of Oblomov 125
South Pacific 107, 111
Sovereign Shopping Centre 141
Squires, Dorothy 103
Squires, Rosemary 100
Stage, The 63
Steffani and his Silver Songsters, Arturo 75

Sterling, Antoinette 18
Stevens, Ernest 35, 36
Stewart, JS 13
Stewart, Jose 105
Stone, Richard 100, 111, 117
Stray, Walter 35
Strelsky and his Russian Cossack Band,
     Captain 64
Stubbs, Philip 143, 144
Stuckey, Lew 104, 107, 108, 111
Summer and Winter Gardens 10
Summer Revellers, The 51, 53, 58, 59, 70
Summer Rhapsody 78, 80
Summer Showboat 126-129
Summer Showtime 142
Summers, Dorothy 70
Sunday Showtime 97, 100
Sutton, Randolph 73, 85, 86, 91
Sweet, The 139

Tait, Jean 57
Tanner, Arthur 18
Tarri, Suzette 78
Teachers, National Union of 29
Thanks for the Memory 91
That'll Be the Day 142
Thomas, Winifred 24
Thorpe, Peter 112
Those Were the Days 107
Tidman, Joyce 111
Titley, Leslie 87, 88
Tivoli Cinema 39, 63
Toogood, Ernest 42
Took, Barry 73
TOPPS Drama Club 140
Tottle, Mr 26
Town Advertising Association (TAA) 26, 35,
     38, 41, 51
Toye, Jennifer 120
Travers, Ben 69
Tremeloes, The 139
Trinder, Tommy 103
Tripp, George 18

Troise and his Mandoliers 74
Tropicana Pleasure Beach 137-139, 147
Troughton, Patrick 69
Tucker, Walter 24
Turner, Edward 51, 77
Twentieth Century Variety Orchestra 64
Twinkle 70
Two Leslies, The 69
Tyler, Keith 88

Uncle Tom's Cabin 22
Upper Church Road Traders' Association 131

Van Buren and Greta 130
van Ost, Valerie 125
Vanbrugh, Irene 55
Vance, Charles 113, 125
Varney, Reg 51, 73
Vaughan, Norman 112, 117, 118
Victoria Hall 8, 10, 15, 17, 34
Victory Vanities 64
Vincent, Robbie 69
Vivian, Mona 48
Voss-Bark, Conrad 111
Vulcaris 18

Waldini and his Gypsy Band 74
Wall, Max 73
Wallace, Edgar 23
Ward, Henry 29
Washington and the Ram Jam Band, Geno
     139, 140
Watts, Bernie 133
Wayfarers Drama Group 111, 113, 125
We Were in the Forces 69, 70
Weedon, Bert 106
We'll Meet Again 69
West, Mae 45
West, Marjorie 96, 99
Western Daily Press 13, 16, 17, 22
Western, JG 23
Weston Bay Yacht Club 142, 143
Weston, Clevedon and Portishead Light

Railway 59
Weston Concert Band 137
Weston Gazette 5, 19, 20, 25, 38, 41, 47, 48, 54, 69, 72, 77, 83
Weston Harriers 8, 38
Weston Mercury 71, 91, 92, 93, 99, 105, 122, 130, 132, 141, 147
Weston Players 38
Weston Repertory Company 55, 63, 64, 66
Weston-super-Mare Amateur Orchestra 8
Weston-super-Mare and District Chrysanthemum Society 20
Weston-super-Mare Borough Council 50, 60, 87
Weston-super-Mare Chamber of Trade 137
Weston-super-Mare Choral Society 31
Weston-super-Mare Civic Society 137, 139, 148
Weston-super-Mare Dramatic Society 6, 24, 39, 51, 52, 64, 111, 113, 150
Weston-super-Mare General Hospital 16, 24, 43
Weston-super-Mare Hotels' and Restaurants' Association 131, 134, 138, 147
Weston-super-Mare Operatic Society 6, 22, 24, 28, 31, 43, 52, 88, 89, 100, 104, 107-109, 111, 114, 121-123, 125
Weston-super-Mare Ratepayers' Protection Association/Weston and District Ratepayers' and Residents' Association/ Weston and Woodspring Ratepayers' Association 25, 30, 121, 131
Weston-super-Mare Rugby Club 9
Weston-super-Mare Town Commissioners 5, 10
Weston-super-Mare Urban District Council 5, 11
Whitecross Hall 61, 86
Wilkin, Gwenda 93, 99
Williams, Bransby 37
Williams, Lauri 103, 108, 116, 130
Williams, Yvonne 82, 106, 108
Wilsher, Doris 86, 87, 89, 92, 107
Wilson, Beatrice 18
Wilson, Edith 81
Wilson, Keppel and Betty 64
Wilton, Robb 6, 78

Winter Gardens/Pavilion 11, 38, 41, 47, 51, 63, 70, 82, 95, 99, 103, 113, 117, 121, 130, 134, 138-142, 144
Wisdom, Norman 6, 71, 73
Wrigg, Ann 57
Woodspring District Council 129, 130, 132, 134, 138, 139, 141-145
Wurzels, The 142
Wyatt, George 85

Yates, Christine 99
Yates, John J 111
Young, Douglas 74, 80
Young, Jimmy 81, 100

Zancig, Agnes and Julius 18